ELITE FLYERS

ELITE FLYERS

THE MEN—THE MACHINES—THE MISSIONS

Andy Evans

ARMS AND
ARMOUR

Arms & Armour Press
An imprint of the Cassell Group
Wellington House, 125 Strand, London WC2R 0BB

Distributed in the USA by Sterling Publishing Co. Inc., 387
Park Avenue South, New York, NY 10016-8810

Distributed in Australia by Capricorn Link (Australia) Pty Ltd,
2/13 Carrington Road, Castle Hill, New South Wales 2154

British Library Cataloguing-in-Publication data:
A catalogue record for this book is available from the British
Library.

ISBN 1 85409 243 X (HBK)
ISBN 1 85409 354 1 (PBK)

Edited and designed by Roger Chesneau/DAG Publications Ltd

Printed & bound in Slovenia by Printing House DELO-Tiskarna
by arrangement with Korotan Ljubljana

CONTENTS

FOREWORD

It hardly seems a moment since the Wright Brothers took to the air at Kitty Hawk, and yet we stand facing a new millennium with some of the most sophisticated and fearsome aerial firepower imaginable.

The appeal of aviation and air combat has both a technical and a human face. Books and films on air power choose one or the other as their basis: they zero in on the blazing speed and sophistication of the aircraft, or they focus on the heroism and skills of the people at the controls. To those of us who fly military aircraft, and to the author of this book, the distinction between man and machine is less clear. We now fly *weapons systems*, blending the power of the aircraft, the speed of computers and the intelligence of men, in unique combinations, to accomplish a particular task. The 'right stuff' may now come from the front seat, the back seat, the flight deck, or the console or cargo compartment—it all depends on the mission.

The range of missions carried out today has exploded since the first powered flight. This evolution is a twentieth-century phenomenon, reflecting the change both in society and in the general conduct of war. Chivalry, simplicity and romance characterized the early days of aviation through to World War One. Technology and industrialization made things more impersonal, driving tactics towards mobility, speed and lethality. Radar, jet engines and advanced avionics made their appearance during World War Two, to support strategic bombardment campaigns as well as the advance of armored columns. During the 1950s and 1960s aerospace engineers continued to refine equipment and theories until they conquered space and fielded the first complete selection of mission-tailored aircraft and weaponry.

Modern developments in aviation are bringing more information into the cockpit, just as television and personal computers bring information into the home. The challenge is no longer to build the fastest

Below: Harrier GR.7—'The Magic'. (Photo: BAe)

Right: 'That others may live': HH-60G Pave Hawk. (Photo: Curtiss Knowles)

Right: Lieutenant-Colonel David Scott, Commanding
Officer, 7th Special Operations Squadron, United States Air
Forces Europe. (USAF)

jets or carry the biggest payload, but to develop the
best sensors, the most powerful computers and the
most intuitive human interface. We are now flying
airplanes that cannot be seen on radar while we
snorkel between hills that cannot be seen without
it, and as we go faster and further with more
precision than before we must not forget that success in war still relies on individual courage and a
clear head.

Someone has to tell the machine what to do and
where to go. This may require tactical genius or just
plain guts, but either way it's the combination of a
specialized airplane and a crew—an élite team, and
one that wins.

David Scott

INTRODUCTION

*E*lite Flyers contains a diverse mixture of aircraft, airmen and air power, yet it reflects a mere brush-stroke on the broad canvas of unique aerial operations that are an integral part of modern warfare. All pilots and crewmen who dare to strap themselves to ejection seats or sit a few feet beneath fast-turning rotors are amongst the élite and are to be admired for their courage and determination. Now, more than ever, these qualities are being put to the test, in combat situations around the globe.

Elite Flyers provides a glimpse into this world, looking at the men, the machines and the missions and investigating the specialities, equipment and fighting capabilities of a number of aircraft types, both fixed-wing and rotary. The particular brand of airmanship of these flyers is described in detail and encompasses such tasks as tanking, A-10 tank-busting, close air support and clandestine operations, from planning to prosecution—seen through the eyes of the flyers themselves. Each brings his own style, authority and sense of humour to the pages, reflecting the professional, dedicated approach he takes to every situation.

Acknowledgements

A publication of this nature would not have been possible without the outstanding support of units and individual airmen who have freely contributed their time and experience. A veritable army of assistants were called upon, and the author wishes to express his sincere thanks to all: Captain Marcella Adams; Major Mike Waters; Mike Kopack; Steve Gensler; Gordon Bartley at British Aerospace; George Heath; Cindy McAllister; McDonnell Douglas; Betty Stephens; Paul J. Perron; Curtiss Knowles; Sqn Ldr Andy Suddards; GEC Ferranti; Flt Lt Bob Chalmers; Andy Hodgson; MSgt Todd Schroeder; Lt-Col Joe Papay; Major Don Kappell; Captain Steve Jacobowski; Karole Scott; Tony Thornborough; Scott Hedglin; MSgt David Brock; Bell Helicopters; Major Kevin Emerson; Major John Greenhalgh; Westland Helicopters; Captain Paul Barton; Chris Shepherd; Dale Donovan; Mark Smith; Ian Stern; Al Dubiel; Julius Alexander; Lockheed; Melissa Bernard; 1/Lt Christopher Holmes; Captain Dennis Nylist; Captain Mark Ramsay; Hal Klopper; and, especially, Mike Verier.

This book is dedicated to my wife Dawn and my children Sarah, Catherine, Alexandra and David.

Andy Evans

Left: A close-up on the AH-64 Apache's Honeywell IHADS system clipped to the pilot's helmet, allowing a 'window' into the gloom, projected through the monocular tube to the right eye. (Photo: McDonnell Douglas)

Right: Head-on Harriers: a good look at the angular FLIR housing atop the radome and the superb visibility offered by the canopy as a four-ship section of 'Plusses' formates, complete with four-round rocket launchers. (Photo: McDonnell Douglas)

TRAINING TO FIGHT

'The students learn to fly the Jaguar at a "geometric rate". It's a very hard and demanding course, especially when they move from the two-seat trainer into the single-seat environment, where the workload can get astronomical at times.' Flight Lieutenant Andy Cubin, a Qualified Flying Instructor (QFI), talks about the means by which the Royal Air Force trains its pilots on the Jaguar GR.1 at Lossiemouth in Scotland, where they get their first taste of 'The Cat' with No 16(R) Squadron, the Jaguar Operational Conversion Unit.

'The Jag is a powerful, twin-engine beast and, despite its age, in aircraft terms is still at the sharp end of operations, both with the RAF and with foreign air arms. It still packs a mighty punch, and its low aspect ratio is designed for high-speed flight, making it a very stable weapons platform. The RAF currently has Jaguars employed in operations over Bosnia, and they have recently completed a long stint of armed recce over Iraq—and of course they proved their worth as the 'Desert Cats' during the Gulf War. Plus, as the Jaguar is the last

Right: The Jaguar GR.1 is the last bastion of single-seat non-VSTOL operations within the RAF and is a prized posting for the ambitious pilot. (Photo: BAe)

single-seat non-VSTOL aircraft on the RAF's inventory, it is a prized posting for an ambitious pilot.

'No 16(R) Squadron takes both *ab initio* and refresher trainees—that is to say, flyers new to the aircraft and established pilots who are returning to flying after other duties or other aircraft. The "long course" for new students is our primary course, taking some four months and 85 hours' flying (depending on the weather) to complete. This gives the student his basics on the aircraft before he moves to Coltishall for a further 4- to 6-month work-up prior to being declared combat-ready.

'We have six GR.1As and six T.2As on strength, and the students use these for initial dual work and then solo sorties. The syllabus is split into phases and we begin with the "CV" phase (Convex Conversion), which includes six simulator trips and systems and ground school before they can get their

Flight Lieutenant Andy Cubin

Andy Cubin ('Cubes') is 32 years old and was born in the Shetland Islands. He has been around aircraft and airfields all his life as his father was a 'Met Man' with the Ministry of Defence. He joined the Royal Air Force at the age of eighteen and took the usual route to fast-jet flying, finally being posted to the Jaguar in 1984. His first operational tour was with No 54 Squadron at RAF Coltishall, before an exchange posting took him to No 20 Squadron in the Sultan of Oman's Air Force. After two years of hot-climate flying he returned to the United Kingdom and gained his QFI rating before returning to Lossiemouth with the OCU. A further opportunity in Oman saw him stationed at Thumrait, training students on the Jaguar; this included the period just prior to, during and immediately after the Gulf War. He returned to the UK, only to find himself posted back to the Gulf as part of Operation 'Warden', in which he flew 88 patrols over Iraq. He returned to the Jaguar OCU in 1993, where he currently holds the post of STANEVAL (Flying) and CFS Agent. During 1994 he was chosen to be the RAF's Jaguar Display Pilot, flying an all-black aircraft at air shows the length and breadth of the country. (Photo: via Andy Cubin)

Above: Andy Cubin at the controls of a Jaguar GR.1 on a low-level 'bounce' sortie, acting as the 'bad guy', during the Evasion phase of the Jaguar course. This provides realistic training for the students and is not staged merely to 'hack them off'. (Photo: Andy Cubin)

hands on a live aircraft. They then strap into a T.2 with an instructor in the back and begin the first of three conversion exercises, ending with a fourth solo slot involving getting airborne, a short, low-level route at 500 feet, a medium-level handling exercise and then back to bash the circuit. That is followed by a formation-flying phase, airborne in pairs, instrument flying, and a preliminary grading. Then a low-level phase begins, with the student learning to operate the aircraft low down, navigating, finding targets and meeting time-on-target requirements. He learns to make decisions on fuel and how to use the INS [inertial navigation system]. We then move to the weapons phase using 3kg smoke-generating "bean-tin bombs", usually dropped over one of the ranges, flying pattern after pattern, initially using level lay-downs, 30-degree shallow-dive deliveries and strafe techniques with the cannons.

'The next phase is the SAP, or Simulated Attack Profile, where we take a bridge or power station or some other structure and simulate it as a target, plan an attack and launch to strike it. Initially this is done as a singleton, but then we move into multi-plane packages. We will also have incorporated an FRA—First Run Attack—on to one of the ranges. So there is a lot of work for the student—lots of planning, timings and teamwork. After that come two trips of Combat at medium level, and to complete SAP is the Evasion phase at low level, in either pairs or a four-ship, with a fifth aircraft, flown by an instructor who acts as the "bounce" or "bad guy". By the end of the course the student will have worked extremely hard . . .

'One of the most involved and demanding sorties flown by the students comes in the Evasion phase and is one of the last they fly with the OCU. It's a four-ship, with a fifth aircraft tasked as the "bounce". The boys will get together two and a half hours before take-off time and be presented with a target, a scenario and current "intel" on the threat area. They will look at troop positions, enemy installations, missile systems etc., and they will then draw up a map, albeit one of Scotland, where we will be using known features as "enemy" positions. For example, Balmoral Castle will be designated a SAM site and Aberdeen a well-defended airfield.

'The target is set as a bridge, and we then build up an intel picture around that. We have a TOT

No 16 (Reserve) Squadron

Originally established at St Omer in France in February 1915, No 16 Squadron has by tradition been associated with the Army, either as a co-operation unit or in the role of ground attack. Between the wars it operated from the United Kingdom, returning to France in 1939. It took on the reconnaissance task for the remainder of the war, and during the post-war period it was a permanent part of the RAF in Germany, flying, in the ground attack role, the Tempest, Vampire, Venom, Canberra, Buccaneer, Jaguar and Tornado GR.1. As part of the 'Options for Change' proposals, No 16 was decommissioned as a Tornado unit and its 'numberplate' was transferred to the Jaguar Operational Conversion Unit (No 226 OCU) at RAF Lossiemouth.

Above: One item of self-defence equipment for the Jaguar is the Phimat chaff dispenser, which was also carried by Harriers operating over Iraq and by Tornado F.3s during the Gulf War. (Photo: Author)

Right: This particular Jaguar has been prepared for service in both the Gulf and Bosnia—witness the overall grey scheme and the tell-tale sand paintwork inside the air brakes. (Photo: Author)

[time on target], and each individual in the four-ship is given his own task during the planning stage, so, provided everyone does his job, nothing should get left out. At the end of a two-hour planning period we should have a fifty-thou Ordnance Survey map which will contain the target within a triangle. Drawn back from that will be the track line and attack direction to the IP [Initial Point], which should be a large feature with some vertical extent and easy to spot, so once the students fly over this feature they can update their INSs, giving accurate steering information to the target. To ensure that they are not totally reliant on the systems, they will also map-read their way using an OS map. As they will be doing seven and a half miles a minute, the ground will go by very quickly, so they will need to look ahead and "navigate at speed" to pick up the target. Once this is acquired,

the idea is to put the weapons aiming symbology in the HUD [head-up display] through the target and simulate weapons release. Each delivery is video-taped and scrutinized later to ensure that the correct procedures have been followed.

'Once the details are sorted, they are transferred to a half-mil map and the route from the IP is drawn back to base. This includes a lot of "corners" in case the formation is late, a circumstance that would allow us to take out a few turns to make up the lost time. The corners are then marked as waypoints and entered into a computer database and then

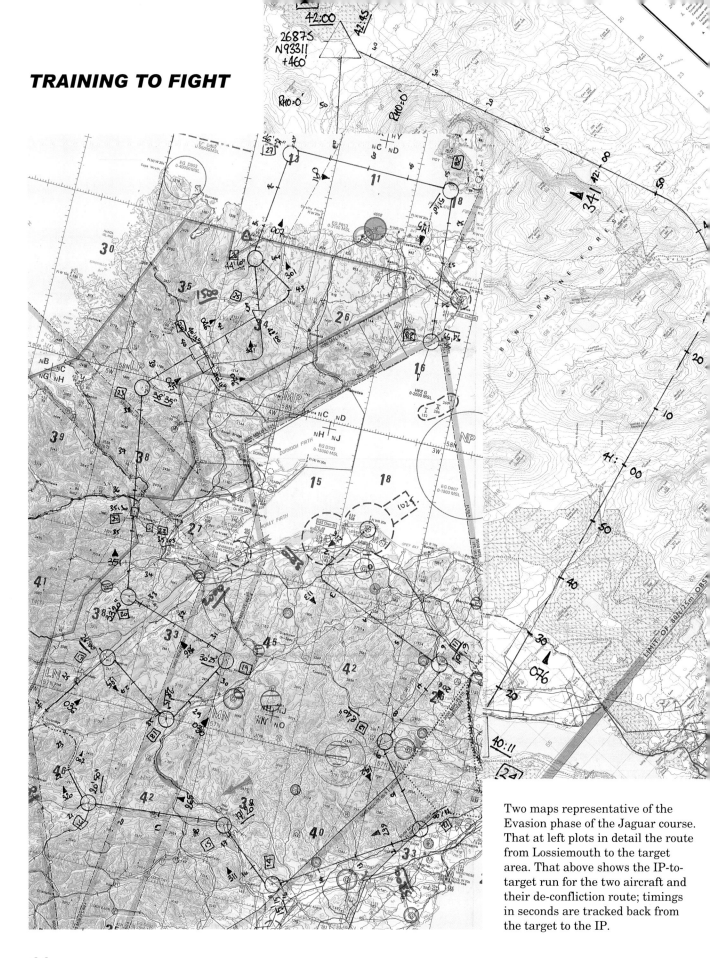

Two maps representative of the Evasion phase of the Jaguar course. That at left plots in detail the route from Lossiemouth to the target area. That above shows the IP-to-target run for the two aircraft and their de-confliction route; timings in seconds are tracked back from the target to the IP.

Right: The Jaguar's 'chisel nose' contains its LRMTS (Laser Ranger and Marked Target Seeker), and here the high set of the aircraft's wings is also very much in evidence. (Photo: Author)

transferred into a "brick", which is essentially a small cartridge that is plugged into the aircraft's own computer and saves having to punch in all the flight information by hand. Additionally the map will contain heading, times, fuel and NOTAMs [Notices to Airmen, i.e. areas to avoid]. Everyone has a copy of the map, and one is left on the desk as a back-up in case one of the formation does not return and also for other flights to use for "de-confliction" with other sorties.

'The crews then take an "outbrief" by the squadron authorizer and pick up their flight kit (which in winter includes a total immersion suit), g-pants and lifejacket. They then move to the line hut, where they sign for the jets and check the "700s" which report the service state of each aircraft. A walk-round is performed and the boys strap into their bang-seats, check their systems and wind up the engines. Once set up, the formation will wait for the leader to check in: "Wildcat 1 . . . 2 . . . 3 . . . 4 . . .", each pilot answering with his assigned number. There will be a frequency hop to "Ground" or "Stud 1", and the leader will call for "Taxy".

'Departure clearance is received and the four-ship lines up on the runway, in two pairs inter-spersed. The leader gives the "wind-up" signal by waving his finger in the air and the aircraft are run up to full dry power. At a predetermined point the leader calls the "hack" to start watches and initiates take-off by chopping his hand on the cockpit coaming. The front pair release brakes and roll for a second or two before the leader gives an exaggerated nod of his head and the re-heat is engaged. The pair steam down the runway and at the rotate point the leader pulls the Jag into the air, followed by the second aircraft, which must match the leader's speed or will otherwise overshoot or drop back. With the pair airborne, gear and flaps come in and the air-conditioning comes on as they accelerate to 450 knots. Fifteen seconds after the leader releases brakes, the second pair get airborne. The formation switches to the departure frequency and, once cleared from Lossiemouth airspace, hop on to "Tactical".

'They then proceed in "card" formation—the basic shape of a number four playing card—which provides good mutual support for all concerned. After following the tactical route they reach a "pre-IP", which is used to update the inertial navigation system and bring the time base back on line if

Above: Practice bomb carriers and wing tanks adorn a pair of grey-clad birds. (Photo: BAe)

Left: Seen after the Gulf War, Andy Cubin's Jaguar Patrol flies low over Mosul airfield in northern Iraq to pay some attention to a MiG-23 that has been noted on a previous mission. The noise impact of the pass is evident from the postures of the ground personnel! (Photo: Andy Cubin)

Right: Andy Cubin on patrol over northern Iraq, in a touched-up aircraft, as part of Operation 'Warden'. (Photo: Andy Cubin)

necessary. This is achieved as we overfly the point by punching the "fix" button on the computer, which then displays the error—which can be cleared or updated. The target run will simulate laying down 1,000lb bombs, and at the final IP a 45-second split between aircraft will be necessary to avoid the following aircraft being hit by the first aircraft's bomb debris. During this time the "bounce" is in the area and can hit at any point. His job is to provide a realistic aid to evasion training, not to "hack off" the formation with his manoeuvres. He will also check that the mutual support is working efficiently. If we see the "bounce" early enough we can "step

around" him and not get involved in a fight, but if the "bounce" gets "in" the remit is to evade effectively by getting a 180 on him and getting inside his missile envelope and running away. So by the time he's turned around, having gone past, the evader has lots of speed and he finds it difficult to acquire us again.

'In the event of the "bounce" getting right into your "shorts" late in the target run, the deal is a "knickers" option. "Knickers" is a code-word for releasing a bomb in the opposition's face: he would be tucked in behind you, tracking, tracking, and about to loose off a missile. So you release a bomb

Top: A Jaguar T.2, used as the basic training/conversion aircraft on the Jaguar course at RAF Lossiemouth. (Photo: Gensler)

Above: During 1994 Jaguars from the United Kingdom were deployed to Italy to support the United Nations 'no-fly zones' over Bosnia. Here a fully armed GR.1 patrols the skies over the war-torn country. (Photo: BAe)

Above right: Despite its age, the Jaguar is still at the sharp end of operations, both in the RAF and in foreign service. The Gulf War saw the addition of overwing missile pylons to the RAF aircraft. (Photo: BAe)

Right: Flying his 'Black Cat', Andy Cubin demonstrates the Jaguar GR.1 in his capacity as the RAF's 1994/95 Display Pilot. (Photo: BAe via Andy Cubin)

to cause an explosion between the two aircraft and he will get caught in the debris hemisphere . . .

'The Jaguar still has good prospects within the RAF. It will soon be fitted with the TIALD [Thermal Imaging Airborne Laser Designation] pod, pioneered by the Tornados in the Gulf, giving us the ability autonomously to prosecute a mission or provide stand-off designation for other aircraft delivering LGBs [laser-guided bombs] from medium altitude.

This task was previously undertaken by the now retired Buccaneers using their Pave Spike system. FLIR [forward-looking infra-red] is also on the horizon, as are NVGs [night vision goggles], giving us a true night fighting capability. Operations over Iraq and Bosnia will see the aircraft retaining their commitment to the strike role, and here at the OCU we will continue to develop and hone the skills of the students who train to fight with the Jaguar.'

HIGH-SPEED BOOMING

High above the green fields of Germany, elements of the Luftwaffe formate with aircraft of the United States Air Force in Europe. In a well-coordinated routine, interdictor/strike (IDS) and Jever-based electronic combat and reconnaissance (ECR) Tornados of JBG-38 fly in line abreast off the port wing of 'Quid Six-Five,' a Boeing KC-135R Stratotanker from the 100th Air Refueling Wing's 351st Air Refueling Squadron, who operate out of RAF Mildenhall, where they are part of the European Tanker Task Force (ETTF). Flying along the well-established 'Dortie' tanker tow-line, the Tornado pilots watch as the snake-like boom is lowered from the rear of the KC-135, carrying at its extremity a drogue basket that will enable their probe-equipped aircraft to take on much-needed fuel.

Below: Larry Westwood stocks *Loaded Dice* with the day's essentials—maps, charts, kit, water and the all-important food boxes. (Photo: Author)

Extending its IFR probe, the first ECR Tornado moves into position, rolling in from the left and lining up with the basket. After a brief aerial ballet with the drogue, a good connection is made and 'Contact' is then called from the tanker. The valves are opened and 3,000lb of fuel is pumped into the fighter's tanks. Three minutes later the aircraft unplugs and falls away to the right, making room for the next customer to make his approach.

For the crew of the KC-135, today is something of a departure from their normal refuelling role, as they would be more used to plugging-in their high-speed boom to a receiver aircraft than trailing a drogue basket. However, being part of the ETTF means that they must practise a different system from that followed by the USAF, and sorties such as this give the tanker crews a valuable insight into these operations—which also allow user air crews to familiarize themselves with the KC-135.

The KC-135 Stratotanker was originally a private-venture aircraft produced by Boeing which made its first flight in 1954, and from these beginnings came the successful 707 airliner. The initial task for the aircraft was to increase the range of the USAF's Strategic Bomber Force, and it has subsequently gone on to serve in a variety of roles and guises. The original KC-135A models were powered by Pratt and Whitney J57-P-59W engines, but many have now been updated with CFM International CFM-56 turbojets, and are re-designated KC-135R, or have been fitted with Pratt and Whitney TF-33-PW-102 turbojets, to become KC-135Es. The 135Rs operated by the ETTF at Mildenhall offer a 50 per cent greater fuel off-load and are 25 per cent more fuel-efficient and therefore cheaper to operate; moreover, they are an amazing 95 per cent quieter than the A models. The operating range for the 'new' E model is in excess of 1,150 miles carrying a 120,000lb fuel off-load.

'Our normal mission would be to gas up aircraft fitted with a receptacle,' comments TSgt Larry Westwood, a boom operator, or 'boomer', with the 351st ARS. 'My job is to "fly" the boom into the

receiver aircraft and monitor the whole tanking procedure from my position at the rear underbelly of the aircraft. The "flying boom" is a very effective method of quickly transferring gas from the tanker; the down side is, of course, that we can only supply one aircraft at a time.

'We are real force-multipliers for the Air Force. We give the fighters and bombers their extra legs for either long-range deployment or exercises, plus we can extend their loiter time in combat or even combat rescue situations, and the fighter guys all

Left: TSgt Larry Westwood lying prone at his boomer's station. The uncomfortable position of the boomer has been addressed on the KC-10, but the strain on his neck is an obvious discomfort. (Photo: Author)

Below: A German Tornado IDS extends its bolt-on IFR probe and positions itself for its turn at the basket. (Photo: Author)

Above: All the ETTF aircraft carry special nose artwork, which serves to give the rather mundane aircraft a little flair. Each of the Stratotankers is very well looked after, both internally and externally. (Photo: Author)

Below: *Loaded Dice* comes to rest on the Mildenhall pan in the late evening sunshine. (Photo: Author)

say that it is a welcome sight to see the tanker, especially if they are coming out of a hostile situation and are getting low on the "go-juice".'

For the five man crew of 'Quid Six-Five', the sortie had begun four hours earlier with a very comprehensive brief, under the authority of Captain Dave Crow, the aircraft commander. One and a half hours later they were out on the hardstand 'pre-flighting' their aircraft, which on this occasion was 3577 *Loaded Dice*, one of Mildenhall's twelve immaculately presented resident tankers. With the hatches closed and checks squared away, Dave Crow is able to start engines on time.

A call to the tower tells the crew that they are ready to roll, and they are given permission to taxi out to the end of Runway One-One. Final clearance is received, and there is a fleeting smell of kerosene as Dave Crow's gloved right hand opens up the throttles. Straining under the power of her four

Above left: The badge of the European Tanker Task Force. (ETTF)

Above centre: The badge of the 351st Air Refueling Squadron.

Above right: The insignia of the 100th ARW, painted on each side of the unit's tankers. (Photo: Author)

CFM-56 engines, 'Quid Six-Five' thunders down the tarmac. At 135kts it passes the important 'S1' point, and with the speed at 172kts the crew rotate, heaving the 294,000lb tanker into the air with a climb gradient set for 5.5 per cent. The gear comes up, and at 192kts the flaps are retracted as the aircraft climbs away to a height of 29,000ft. Taking a radar vector, the crew takes the aircraft to its destination via 'Mike Charlie Six', a reporting point out over the sea. The trip out to the 'Dortie' tow-line takes an hour, routing via RAF Bruggen and descending to 19,000ft when the track is reached. 'Quid Six-Five' is set to spend some three hours on station, with the ability to offload 54,000lb of fuel.

Now settled on the first 'leg' of the tow-line, Larry Westwood walks the length of the aircraft and scrambles down into his cramped work station at its rear. He makes himself as comfortable as possible, lying face down on a red leather 'couch' and placing his chin on a fabric-covered support. In front of him is an optically flat window through which he can view proceedings, and below that is a control panel that shows all the necessary instruments at his disposal. Underneath his couch, at his right hand, is the control stick that will be used for flying the high-speed boom.

'Fighters coming in,' announces Dave Crow. 'Two miles. They're all yours, boom.' Larry Westwood moves the lever to the left of his panel and the boom lowers, the drogue basket extending as it reaches its limits. The first of the Tornados rolls in beneath the tanker and Westwood uses his controller to place the basket at the most advantageous angle for the receiver aircraft. He begins to talk the pilot on to the basket, giving him distances and lots of encouragement. A nudge with the probe and contact is made.

'The boom is like a mini-aeroplane,' explains Larry Westwood. 'It has power elevators fitted to it, which allow me to "fly" the boom using a hand controller. The receiver formates beneath the tanker using a series of lights and position strips on our underside to make his approach, he opens up his receptacle and I fly the boom in. When the tip makes contact with the receptacle it locks in place and I get a contact light on my panel, as does the flight engineer who controls the flow of fuel. The

> ### 351st Air Refueling Squadron
> The 351st ARS has a proud heritage that comes from the 351st Bombardment Squadron, a Second World War unit which was activated in 1942, operated from Thorpe Abbots, some 40 miles from its present home at Mildenhall, and flew the B-17 across France, Italy and Germany. Today the 351st is the only Air Refueling Squadron on permanent assignment in Europe, and it represents USAFE's vital lifeline to military operations. The Squadron has so far supported Operations 'Provide Comfort', 'Provide Promise', 'Restore Hope' and 'Deny Flight' in addition to being the foundation of the European Tanker Task Force. Each of the Squadron's aircraft proclaims the heritage of its combat-proven Second World War Two predecessor: the 'Squared D' of the 100th Bomb Group, to which the 351st belonged, can be seen displayed on the tails of the KC-135 tankers as a reminder of bygone glories.

boom gives us two main advantages: first, faster fuel flow and therefore less time at the tanker, and secondly it's easier to use in turbulent conditions.

'Some aircraft are more demanding to "boom" than others. The F-4, for example, which has only a small receptacle on its spine that opens upwards, is a real challenge, especially at night, whereas something like a C-5 has a huge steel "trash can" and the boom just drops right in.

'Being a "boomer" is something that I have done now for the past fourteen years,' concludes Westwood. 'The prone position we adopt is pretty taxing on your neck muscles after a while, and it can get pretty cold down in the bottom of the aircraft sometimes, but where else can you pass gas all day—and get paid for it!'

Left: The C-5 'has a huge steel "trash can" and the boom just drops right in'. (Photo: Knowles)

Right, upper: Having failed at his first attempt to 'prod' the basket, the pilot drops back for another go. (Photo: Author)

Right, lower: To achieve a fuel-flow the receiver aircraft must first 'push' the drogue basket forward to open the internal valve, as this close-up photograph demonstrates. (Photo: Author)

HIGH RISK—HIGH PAY-OFF

'I t's the largest, meanest and most powerful helicopter in the US Air Forces inventory. Also it just happens to be the most technologically advanced helo in the world, and is exclusively operated by the Special Operations Command'—enthusiastic comments about the unique Sikorsky MH-53J Pave Low III Enhanced by Captain Tim Brown of the 21st SOS, the 'Dust Devils', based at RAF Alconbury in England. 'This aircraft gives us the capability to go into any situation, low-level, undetected, at night or in bad weather, hugging the terrain and using unprepared landing zones or operating off of carriers or assault ships.

'Pave Low was developed as a result of Operation "Eagle Claw", the attempt to rescue American hostages from the US Embassy in Teheran in 1980. During this combined operation, only one of eight Navy RH-53D Sea Stallion helicopters, flown by Marine pilots, carrying Army units, survived. Crews had to fly through sandstorms using only their altimeters, attitude direction instruments and DR navigation; as a result they became exhausted and disorientated—factors that doubtless contributed to the sad losses at the "Desert One" site.

'In the aftermath of the débâcle, the Holloway Commission was established to review the events.

Right: 'It's the largest, meanest and most powerful helicopter in the US Air Forces inventory.' (Photo: Sikorsky)

One of their recommendations was to develop a night-capable, low-level, "infil/exfil" penetration aircraft. The Air Force already had the HH-53C Super Jolly Green Giant in service, and this was being used to rescue downed airmen; they also had a number of modified CH-53C Pave Knife models being utilized by Special Operations Command (having already gained fame in a number of incidents, including Operation "Frequent Wind"). It was recommended that these aircraft, 41 in all, should undergo an extensive modification programme called Project "Pave Low" and be subsequently re-assigned to AFSOC as "new" MH-53J Pave Low III Enhanced models.

'Externally, most of the modifications can be found at the nose of the helicopter. It has an IFR probe, radar and FLIR all housed in various lumps and bumps that do nothing for the aircraft's appearance but do wonders for its abilities! Central to the Pave Low's capabilities is an excellent mission computer, coupled to the INS and doppler navigation systems with a projected moving-map display and Global Positioning System. The radar is a

Captain Tim Brown
Captain Tim Brown (far left), Pave Low helicopter pilot with the 21st Special Operations Squadron and a veteran of many missions during the Gulf War. More recently he has been operating from Incirlik in Turkey in support of United Nations efforts.

TSgt Mario Roiz
TSgt Mario Roiz, left, is an 'Engineer in the Seat' with 21 SOS. (Photos: Author)

Left: The cockpit of the Pave Low is filled with electronic wizardry that allows it to prosecute clandestine missions. The FLIR screens are prominent, situated in front of the pilots. (Photo: Author)

Below left: The 'night window' of the Pave Low, the FLIR, is here rolled back in its ball housing. (Photo: Author)

Below centre: Pave Low's range is virtually unlimited, by virtue of its IFR probe: in fact, time spent aloft is governed solely by the endurance of the crew. (Photo: Author)

multi-mode AN/APQ-158 TF/TA (which can be coupled to the autopilot) and allows the helicopter to operate dangerous NOTE (nap of the earth) flying at speeds in excess of 170kts at 150ft, in visibility as low as a quarter of a mile—a feature that can drop the aircraft to below 100ft over water or in desert conditions. The other main night sensors consist of a Texas Instruments AN/AAQ-10 FLIR fitted in a ball turret under the nose and the routine use of night vision goggles, worn by all crew members.

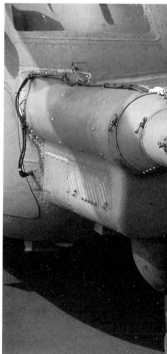

The Pave Low has its own self-protection devices in the shape of two Loral AN/ALQ-157 IRCMs mounted on the external fuel tank sponsons directly beneath the engine exhausts, and a number of chaff and flare dispensers located at the rear and on the forward underside of the fuselage. Unrefuelled range has also been improved by the addition of two 400-gallon drop tanks, and the crew also benefit from 1,000lb of armour plate plus titanium seats to protect the pilots.

'The Pave Low has a crew of six, two officers and four enlisted men,' continues Tim Brown. 'The pilot/aircraft commander occupies the right-hand seat, the co-pilot the left. A flight engineer sits between them and it is his job to look after all of the cockpit. A second flight engineer sits in the back and he is in charge of the cabin and also acts as right scanner. We have two aerial gunners (one of whom acts as left scanner, one as tail scanner), and they are in charge of the three 7.62mm machine guns which are mounted on shock-absorbing pedestals fitted inside the rear ramp or in the windows. A recent addition has been to install floor-mounted ammunition boxes to better feed the guns, which are each capable of spraying 4,000 rounds per minute. Typically we are able to carry 37 combat troops, sixteen litters, vehicles, boats or around 20,000lb of externally hung cargo.'

Apart from the intensive aspects of flying the helicopter, one of the pivotal roles within the Pave Low is fulfilled by the flight engineer located on the flight deck, or the 'Engineer in the Seat' as he is called. SSgt Mario Roiz explains: 'The mantle of flight engineer means he is loadmaster, radio operator, gunner or winchman. In fact he's the "jack of all trades" on the '53. On the flight deck he watches the radar and the TF/TA display, monitors the instruments and the RWR and reads off the checklists. If the pilot wants a take-off check, the "Engineer in the Seat" takes it; if he wants the pre-landing check, again the "Engineer in the Seat" accomplishes it. Nothing is taken on or off the aircraft without the engineer knowing.

Below: Central to the Pave Low's low-level attributes is its excellent AN/APQ-158 TF/TA radar. (Photo: Author)

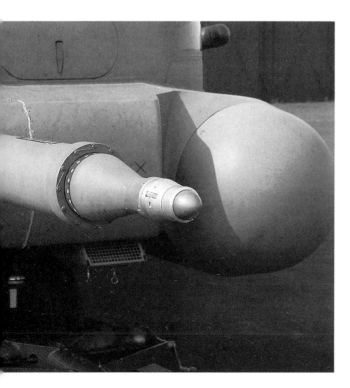

Above: Pave Low power. The aircraft is 'for its size . . . a very agile helicopter.' (Photo: Mark Smith)

Above right: Kicking up a grass storm, a 'European One'-camouflaged aircraft carries out a 'dust off' landing with its ramp down ready to 'exfil' troops. (Photo: Mark Smith)

Below: A grey-camouflaged MH-53J Pave Low. Its warty appearance belies its capabilities. (Photo: Author)

'We can fly the '53 with a minimum crew of two pilots and an engineer, but they can't fly at all without an engineer! Our flight preparation begins with being told our aircraft. The engineer goes out and does the weights and balance and checks that the '53 has the correct configuration. He does the performance data, makes sure the aircraft is within

21st Special Operations Squadron

The 21st SOS originated as the 21st Pursuit Group on 21 December 1939 and the unit became involved with rotary-wing operations during 1956 at Donaldson AFB flying the H-21. Reorganization saw the unit reappear at Shaw AFB in 1967 on the CH-3 before it moved to Nakhon Phanom RTB in late 1967, flying infil/exfil operations, SAR and airlift. The Squadron converted to the CH-53 in 1970 and participated in the final evacuation of Saigon in 1975. The unit also provided infil/exfil airlift for the US Marines in their attempt to rescue the crew of the SS Mayaguez. With MH-53s, the unit has since then served in Germany and the United Kingdom, taking part in 'Desert Storm', 'Proven Force', 'Provide Comfort', 'Provide Comfort II' and 'Provide Promise'.

limits and then returns to update the pilot. He attends the main mission briefing, at which the pilot gives him the nav-log, and once he is released he collects his survival gear, flight kit and body armour (if necessary) and goes out to "pre-flight" the aircraft. He gets all the systems on line and readies the radar, so when the pilots walk out all they have to do is start the engines. The engineer reads out the checklists; the pilots respond; they start the engines; the engineer monitors their performance and is then the focal point of the mission, should anything need to be done.'

The cockpit is laid out in a 'T' pattern with pilot and co-pilot having duplicated instruments with primary information displayed down a centre console. Within this centre section are the basic engine and transmission instruments. Directly in front of the crew is the FLIR sensor screen and to the left or right (dependent on seat) is the radar scope—'just like in a James Bond movie,' comments Tim Brown. To the left of the pilot's seat is the very useful 'hover coupler/transfer' stick, which allows the pilot to hover the aircraft accurately above the ground using small inputs from the control. (A further hover coupler is located in the forward crew door, allowing the winchman to control certain delicate

situations: 'We can hit the guy we are rescuing on the head with the hoist if we want.') Below that, on the centre console, is the FLIR control stick, or 'bullpup,' complete with 'Chinaman's hat' for fine-tune control. Just above the centre section is the moving-map display and in the central area are the controls for the enhanced navigation systems, to the right of which can be found a small keyboard for the doppler. Above the doppler is a control panel for the personal locator system, with its display unit mounted above the centre of the main console.

'We generally get our mission tasks well in advance,' continues Tim Brown. 'That can give us that added edge to prepare. We have a new piece of kit to aid our planning called SOFPARS (Special Operations Force Planning and Rehearsal System), which enables us to input our mission into its database and literally "fly" the sortie on a TV screen. It will indicate any known threats or where threats could potentially be located. So we can plan our trip and then spend a few hours going through the more critical phases. For us the most crucial part of any trip is the last mile! So, we can build up a picture of what we should expect to see; of course, it doesn't show population centres, but it gives a good indication of our route.

HIGH RISK—HIGH PAY-OFF

'One of the "plus" factors with Special Ops is the time we have to plan our missions, and for long-range operations we have the ability to use "floating airfields" and air-to-air refuelling. We could be tasked with landing a force at night inland from a beach-head, which would mean our using both airborne and seaborne support.'

With the crew briefed and the helicopter up and running, the engines are pushed to 105 per cent and, heavy with fuel, the Pave Low performs a rolling take-off and heads away into the dusk. 'The first major event of the mission is to meet up with one of the 67th SOS's Hercules tankers over the ocean,' continues Tim Brown. 'The range of the Pave Low is governed solely by the endurance of the crew.

'It always amazes me that after a little preparation a few days before the trip, at the appointed ARCP (air refuelling control point), out of the blackness looms the tanker! From our established altitude we pitch up to 500ft to join the Herc. He will either meet us head-on, racing around behind us in a tight loop, throttling back with flaps down to match our speed, eventually settling 300ft above us; or he could already be established above us, in which case we pitch up from the rear. The probe is extended and we pull up to just below the trailing baskets, and with a little effort make a solid contact.

'We did tank as low as 500ft during "Desert Storm", and, believe me, from our usual operating height of 100ft, 500ft seemed a long way up and very exposed—and some guys gassed up at 100ft too! Tanking complete, our next task, having got back down, is to meet a Marines amphibious assault ship, from where we will launch the second phase of our mission. The Marines are well versed in handling the '53 as they routinely operate the Sea Stallion version. Having found the ship, we are quickly down and are spotted on the deck. Our Pave Lows have now been fitted out for shipboard use with folding rotors and tail unit.

Left: Not an MH-53 but an HH-53H: still, the 'fast rope' techniques are the same. Note the .50-calibre ramp-mounted gun. (Photo: 'Snuffy')

Above right: The 'fast rope' technique is demonstrated here as troops 'exfil' from the giant hovering helo. Ropes can be laid from the rear ramp or crew doors, and 'a full load of troops can be out in around twenty seconds'. (Photo: Mark Smith)

'We may now have a few days to wait for the right time, but when the call comes it's back into the night sky. The radar is able to see up to 40 miles out, but, not wanting to announce our presence too early, we use the FLIR, NVGs and navigational systems to put us into the slot. As we approach the beach-head at a mere 100ft, not wanting to fly higher than we could fall, the TF/TA is engaged to take us over the terrain ahead as low as possible and put us into the DZ [Drop Zone].

'You have to learn to trust the TF,' admits Tim Brown. 'In the back the gunners are scanning for threats with their NVGs and our cargo of troops are getting twitchy. On the flight deck the TF/TA, FLIR and RHWR are under constant scrutiny and over the intercom the conversation is intense. The "Engineer in the Seat" is watching the climb/dive commands and calling what he sees on the radar and PMD [projected map display]. The weapons are ready, the gunners having already test-fired them over the water. Mounted on the windows and ramp are our three GE GAU-2A/B 7.62mm miniguns. They are excellent for throwing out a lot of bullets fast, and we could mount armour-piercing 50mm guns if necessary. One thing we try to explain to other forces is that we are not a gunship—the weapons are for self-protection only!'

With the crew keeping a close eye on the FLIR, the Pave Low reaches its assigned DZ, and with a quick 'dust off' the helo lands. Within seconds the troops deploy, the engines are wound up again and the aircraft heads back out into the night. 'We prefer to land in order to offload our teams,' continues Tim Brown, 'but we can also get them out from the hover using "fast ropes". Out of the helo we can run two lines from the cargo ramp and one from the door, and a full load of troops can be out in around twenty seconds.' The scenario may call for the helo to remain on the ground if the team are expected back, and in that case the crew spend a nervous time scanning for threats as the Pave Low sits with its rotors turning in the blackness.

'In bad-guy territory its good to have a system like Pave Low,' concludes Tim Brown. 'In the Gulf we not only rescued downed airmen but led the first strike of "Desert Storm", when several Pave Lows acted as pathfinders for the Army Apaches who took down the Iraqi early warning radar sites. It's a high risk, high pay-off aircraft, and one that I am proud to fly.'

'SNAKE BITE'

'**S**pecifically, the SuperCobra provides the Marines with point target/anti-armour operations (OAS) and armed escort (helicopter and surface assault support). It also conducts armed and visual reconnaissance and anti-helicopter operations (AAW) and provides a limited area air defence from threats such as fixed-wing aircraft. It can also provide terminal control for friendly fighters or attack aircraft. An extraordinary range of abilities that really proves that the SuperCobra is one of the most versatile and powerful attack helicopters in the world.' High praise indeed, given by Captain Frank H. Simmonds Jr, who flies the Bell AH-1W ('Whiskey') SuperCobra with Marine Light/Attack Helicopter Squadron 269 (HMLA-269), 'The Gunrunners', operating out of MCAS New River in South Carolina.

Frank Simmonds, call-sign 'Zoid', continues: 'In the SuperCobra, both pilot (rear seat) and co-pilot/gunner (front seat) are designated Naval Aviators, and we routinely conduct training missions from both perspectives. The aircraft is very agile, and for its size very powerful. Visibility from the front seat is excellent, and it's pretty good from the back seat too, although the view forward is partially obstructed by the front seat and the Aircraft Survivability Equipment (ASE).

'The mission workload is heaviest in the rear station: this is due to that position having responsibility for the primary flight controls, communications and navigation equipment—plus most of the weapons system selection and trouble-shooting takes place there. Also, with the exception of the very latest models which have an INS, there is no terrain flight navigation system (TERF); consequently the use of pilotage and dead-reckoning has increased the mission workload. Our Squadron has worked round this, however, by purchasing handheld GPS units for use in flight lead aircraft to aid in TERF navigation.

'The SuperCobra is truly an effective weapons platform, and we can carry a lethal mix of ordnance. Dependent on the mission, we are able to choose from a wide selection of armament, which includes the deadly TOW missile (Basic Range and Extended Range), Improved TOW, TOW-2 and TOW-2A. Hellfire laser-guided missiles can also be carried, as can AIM-9 Sidewinders, Sidearm anti-radar missiles and 2.75in rockets containing either high-explosive fragmentation (HE-FRAG), HE anti-tank (HEAT), anti-personnel (AT/APERS), HE general-purpose (GP), flechettes, smoke or flares. Also 5-inch Zuni rockets can be "strapped on", and these can contain GP, AT/APERS, HE-FRAG and chaff.

'We also pack ammunition fired from both the 750-round turret-mounted M-197 20mm gun and the 300-round externally hung gun-pods. These shells can be HEI, HEI tracer, semi-armour-piercing high-explosive incendiary (SAPHEI), target

Marines AH-1W SuperCobra

Right: Frank Simmonds checks over his AH-1W before a mission from New River. Note the Huey in the background. (Photo: Author)

Below: Causing more than a few 'ripples', a Hellfire-equipped Cobra takes up an attack position. (Photo: Bell Helicopters)

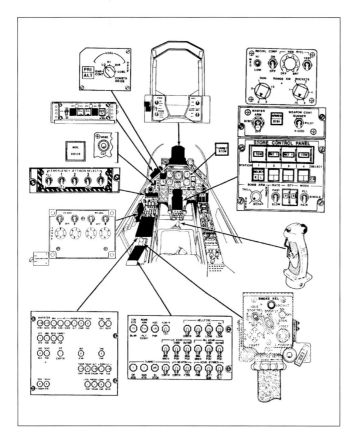

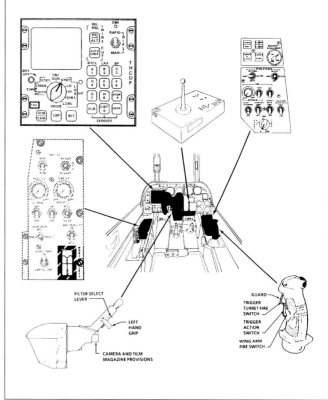

Above: Pilot armament controls (left) and gunner armament controls and indicators (right). (US Navy)

practice (TP) or TP tracer. Additionally we can tote fire bombs (napalm), fuel–air explosive bombs (FAE), and, if necessary, paraflares. Quite an encyclopedia of destruction!

'Power for the SuperCobra comes from two General Electric T700-401 turboshafts, which give us a 65 per cent increase in performance. Protection is provided by armour plating around the crew, able to withstand 23mm shell hits, and we also have on board a dual AN/ALQ-144 IR jammer and overwing ALE-39 chaff and flare dispensers.'

Impressive though the weaponry is, the greatest shortcoming is the SuperCobra's limited night fighting capability. Unlike the Lynx, the SuperCobra does not yet have any sort of thermal image intensifier attached to its TOW system. TOW sighting in the AH-1W is by direct view—that is, the optics are

located in the nose of the helicopter, in line of sight with the front-seater, rather than being mounted on the roof. Still containing the 2x and 13x magnification, this means that unless the enemy is practising very poor light discipline, flares must be used to engage targets after dark. As it stands, it is a viable system for pre-planned missions, but it is difficult to engage targets of opportunity on the battlefield. A further shortfall is the lack of a laser designator, and this increases the requirement for external co-ordination and prevents the aircraft from operating autonomously. These problems are currently being addressed with the SuperCobra Night Targeting System (NTS), which was due to enter service in late 1994. This will provide the aircraft with a laser and much improved night target acquisition/engagement facilities using a FLIR, and will feature enhanced cockpit management systems which will enable the co-pilot/gunner to operate the comms and nav systems.

'Switchology in the front seat centres around the TOW/Hellfire control display panel (THCDP),' continues Frank Simmonds. 'This is located to the left-hand side of the co-pilot/gunner's instrument panel. The telescopic sight unit (TSU) dominates the middle of the cockpit, and this provides the optics for the turret-mounted gun and TOW missiles, and its movement "joystick" is located to the right of the TSU. The helmet-mounted sighting system (HSS) controls and wing pylon fire button can be found on the front seater's cyclic control. Switchology for the rear seat moves around the pilot's stores control and armament control panels, which are located between his legs. The AIM-9 cockpit control unit (CCU) is on the left side of the pilot's glare shield. The Hellfire control panel is located on the left side of the instrument panel, as are the controls for the pilot's HSS. The AIM-9 cage/uncage/fire switch is to be found on his collective control stick, with the trigger and wing pylon arm/fire buttons mounted on his cyclic control.'

TOW missiles can only be employed from the front seat, and the system is very easy to operate. Because it is semi-automatic command line-of-sight (SACLOS), it requires the gunner simply to keep

Above right: The sharp end. The sighting system on the SuperCobra is by 'direct-view' optics, unlike helos such as the Lynx and Warrior, which use mast-mounted sights. This makes the aircraft that much more vulnerable. (Photo: Author)

Right: Once in their seats, the crew strap in and, as demonstrated here by Frank Simmonds in the rear seat, make the connections for their HSS. (Photo: Author)

the target in his optical cross-hairs. He makes the missile selection using his THCDP. The pilot then manoeuvres the Cobra into pre-launch parameters which are displayed in his HUD, and once these are met the missile can be fired. The pilot has to maintain these parameters using his TOW sighting unit (TSU), which means keeping the aircraft within a post-launch 'box' that is displayed in his HUD. TOW wire cut occurs at impact or after a pre-set period of time.

Hellfire missiles can be fired from either position, although the laser codes and missile selection must still be made using the THCDP in the front seat. Again, since the SuperCobra does not have its own laser designation, other ground or air forces must act on its behalf. However, missile ranges of over 8,000m do allow the helicopter to remain masked and away from the danger area.

"The AIM-9 is controlled and fired from the rear seat and has the highest priority in the databus of the weapons sub-system. The symbology is displayed in the HUD and can be locked in line with the aircraft's datum. Once the target is "locked on", the missile is "uncaged" to follow the heat source. Procedures for Sidearm are identical to the AIM-9. Rockets can be fired from either seat using the wing arm fire button, with the rocket selection being made from the rear seat. This selection includes the number of rockets fired with each depression of the fire button. The man in the rear seat also has a rocket aim reticle displayed in his HUD. The turret-mounted 20mm gun can also be fired from either seat using the HSS. Mechanical and electrical attachments on our helmets enable either of us to aim at the target we are viewing. The rear seat can also fire the gun in a fixed forward mode for

Capt Frank Simmonds Jr
Frank Simmonds currently serves as an Attack Helicopter Commander. He began his operational career with HMLA-167 and was detached to HMM-264 for a tour in the Mediterranean that included contingency operations off the coast of the Lebanon. After returning to the United States he re-joined HMLA-167 before being transferred to HMLA-269 as the latter deployed to Saudi Arabia for 'Desert Storm'. After the war he was posted to the Amphibious Warfare Center at Quantico, Virginia, before joining HMM-162, with which he participated in Operations 'Provide Promise' and 'Deny Flight', and in Operation 'Restore Hope' in Somalia. In the photograph, Frank Simmonds and James Jenkins pose in the full flight kit used by the Marines for attack helicopter crews. (Photo: Author)

more effective diving fire or strafing. The front-seater is also able to fire the gun using his TSU, which at 13x mag is the most accurate delivery mode for the weapon. The HSS also aids rapid target acquisition, and the pilot may fire at a "pop-up" target to quickly suppress it while the co-pilot/gunner slaves the TSU to the pilot's line of sight for a more accurate delivery.

'In a time of crisis, the SuperCobra's tasking would originate from the Tactical Air Commander, and aircraft sorties would be determined by threat. Once air superiority had been established, aircraft

HMLA-269
HMLA-269 is one of the US Marine Corps' primary light attack helicopter squadrons. The unit is based at MCAS New River in South Carolina, and is known by the title 'The Gunrunners'. The illustration at left is of an actual unit patch.

Below: : Armed with rocket pods, an AH-1W trolls for 'trade'. (Photo: Mike Verier)

Bottom: A camouflage variation for the AH-1W is this light grey/blue scheme. The helicopter seen here is leaving March AFB in California. (Photo: Author)

Below: The AH-1W carries one of the most varied ranges of armament of any attack helicopter; it is also the only aircraft currently able to carry TOW and Hellfire missiles simultaneously. This one is armed with rocket pods, TOW and Hellfire and gun—'Quite an encyclopedia of destruction!' (Photo: Bell Helicopters)

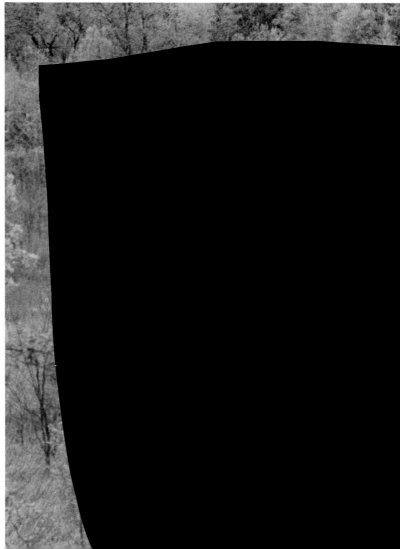

AH-1W SuperCobra
In 1980 a modified Bell AH-1T was test-flown with uprated engines as part of a programme to develop an attack helicopter for the Marines with a much enhanced operational capability. From this test-bed emerged the 'SuperCobra': originally called AH-1T+, it was redesignated AH-1W and is currently the most advanced of the Cobra family in service. The AH-1W has been the Marines' main battlefield attack helicopter since 1986 and is qualified to fire more types of weapon than any other helicopter in the world. It is also unique in its dual anti-armour role, in that, to date, it is the only attack helicopter that can carry TOW and Hellfire missiles simultaneously. (Photo: Bell Helicopters)

will be allotted a certain number of tasks for CAS, or, in Marine speak, "close-in fire support" (CIFS). The GCE will request missions at fixed times-on-target and PPSMs (pre-planned/scheduled missions) or request aircraft to be available during certain PPOCMs (pre-planned/on-call missions). On-call missions can be fulfilled by strip-alert or airborne-alert aircraft. The Direct Air Support Center can ... aircraft assigned to other sorties ... tactical ... CAS".

... e set ... NVG ... n that ... combat ... ection) ... a four-... ting by ... aircraft ... nd two ... (Flare ... who will ... checks ... Nomex ... ypically ... aircraft; ... e neces-... from the ... strap in

'Prior to take-off we conduct radio checks with our mission aircraft. Our first transmissions will be to the DASC, passing our status and receiving our route, altitude, restrictions and intel and the FAC's call-sign and frequency. After obtaining taxi clearance we hover out to the runway, conducting power checks as we go. We take off by section, and RV with the flight en route. Once clear of the "field" we descend to our operational altitude and contact the Tactical Air Operations Center (TAOC) with our IFF [identification friend/foe] codes, and then reapprise the DASC of our current position and get any updates from them. We also test-fire our guns at this time. At the designated contact point we call

up the FAC on his tactical frequency, again passing our status, and we receive from him the standard "nine-line brief".

'The FAC assigns us a run-in to the target, trying to prevent fractricide and getting our weapons parallel to friendly forces. He may be using a MULE (Modular Universal Laser Equipment); if so he will assign us a laser pulse repetition frequency (PRF), so that we in turn can assign the missile codes through the THCDP. Our thorough briefing of actions in the objective area reduces the in-flight communications, having identified in advance the target priorities—which aircraft will fire first, and from which direction. We now squeeze down and, again using NOTE techniques and TERF profiles, we orientate ourselves to the surroundings, using our NVGs to identify any key terrain features. Internal comms centre at this time around verifying weapons settings, sighting friendly positions and double-checking our TOT.'

The TOW-armed Cobras establish themselves at the attack position (AP) and the designated Flare Section manoeuvres out to fire its rocket flares. Once ready to mount the attack, the lead aircraft will call for 'Sunshine', at which point the Flare Section ripple off their illuminators, announcing their launch with a 'Flares away' call. They move

out and reposition at another fire zone. The gunners of the TOW Section now solely concentrate on their TSUs or 'go into the bucket', starting their detailed search for targets.

'Having identified a target that is within missile range, the gunner calls "Ready to fire" to the pilot. He now manoeuvres the aircraft to ensure that the TSU indicator in his HUD is within pre-launch parameters. Once met, the gunner squeezes the trigger on his left-hand grip and announces "Missile away!" The first shot comes off the right-hand side and the pilot looks away to his left to minimize the flash glare in his NVGs, and he acknowledges the missile launch. He then begins timing the shot to verify distance to target, using the missile's time of flight (TOF). The gunner continues to track the round until impact. A check that the wire is cut, and he immediately searches and selects another target as the pilot moves to another firing position. This is repeated by both aircraft in the TOW Section until they either run out of targets—or run out of TOWs!

'The TOW and Flare Sections then make a NOTE egress, joining up at a pre-arranged RV. The FAC passes BDA to us as we leave the area and in turn this feeds to the DASC for an update of intel. They then give us an exit route to the north, and home.'

Left: The stores and self-defence dispensers are mounted on two stub wings which are able to tote an unenviable range of weaponry. In this photograph the chaff/flare 'boxes' are yet to be filled. (Photo: Author)

Right: Rather reminiscent of the Fourth of July, a SuperCobra fires off a salvo of flares from its twin AN/ALE-39 chaff/flare dispensers—enough to ward off even the most determined seeker head. (Photo: Bell Helicopters)

BATTLE CATS

Masked behind a tree line, close to the Forward Edge of the Battle Area (FEBA), an Army Air Corps 'aviation reconnaissance patrol' picks out a couple of 'enemy' tanks trying to establish a forward position. On the ground 1 and 19 Brigades—part of 3(UK) Division—are fighting a covering action to allow 5 Brigade and another part of 19 Brigade to prepare defensive positions; and enemy forces are consolidating themselves near the town of Calne (GR0069). Using their observation skills, the crew of the recce patrol's Gazelle AH.1 assess the situation and report their findings.

Some fifteen miles behind the Gazelle, at a forward re-arming and refuelling point (FARP), the information is received and an anti-tank flight is made ready and tasked to deal with the situation. The anti-tank flight (which is itself part of an anti-tank regiment, containing the scout Gazelle) comprises two powerful Westland Lynx AH.7 helicopters, each of which is armed with eight deadly TOW missiles. These aircraft are field-briefed and then dispatched with urgency to the battle position (BP).

The lead aircraft is crewed by Major Peter Terrett, OC 671 Squadron AAC, with WO2 John McHale as his air gunner. On this occasion it is not war, but all

Major Peter Terrett
Peter Terrett began his flying career in 1985, and after graduating from the Army Flying Course he was posted to Northern Ireland, where he ran No 655 Squadron's Gazelle Flight. After converting to the Lynx, he returned to Ireland again with No 655's Lynx Flight. He then moved to Cyprus, flying the Alouette before once again being posted to Northern Ireland to become 2IC of No 655 Squadron. In 1989 he moved back the mainland Britain with No 3 Regiment in North Yorkshire. At the end of 1990 he took his QHI course at Shawbury and moved to Middle Wallop in February 1991 to take command of No 671 Lynx Flight, before taking overall control of the Squadron in 1992.

Above: A TOW missile moments after launch speeds toward its target. Provided the air gunner keeps the cross-hairs on his prey, the round is guaranteed to hit. (Photo: Westland)

Left: Flying low and fast sees the Lynx in its element. It is 'one of the best anti-tank helicopters in the world', and its robust characteristics can be seen here as Peter Terrett speeds toward the battle position. (Photo: Author)

part of an intensive 'Cool Hand' exercise into which the flyers of the Army Air Corps are pitched, in order to hone their skills, for one of these days it may be for real . . .

The Lynx/TOW and Gazelles form part of the Army's Joint Air Attack (JAAT) strategy, an updated concept in aerial warfare which reflects the changing face of today's Air Corps operations. 'What

was a "threat-driven" Army is now a "capability-driven" Army,' explains Major John Greenhalgh of the Tactics Wing at the Army Air Corps Centre at Middle Wallop. 'With the perceived threat no longer coming from the Soviet Union, but from any corner of the world, today's Army and its Air Corps must align themselves to this new order.

'The Lynx/TOW is the centrepiece of our attack capabilities,' continues John Greenhalgh. 'We believe that it is one of the best anti-tank helicopters in the world. It has the payload, it has the range, it's rugged and in possession of all the right characteristics for an attack platform. Within the Anti-Tank Squadron we field six Gazelles and six Lynx/TOW helicopters. These are further divided into two armed reconnaissance units, a tactical unit, a close air support flight, an anti-tank flight and a gun flight.

'The Lynx/TOW has an excellent sighting arrangement with the optics mounted on the cab roof above the left-hand seat. (All Army Air Corps helicopters are generally referred to as "cabs".) The sight includes not only a daylight visual 2.5x or 13.5x sight, but also a thermal imager (TI) for night-time operations. The thing about TI is that it's just as useful in daylight as it is at night. That is to say, it's sometimes quicker to find a target using TI because it's hot; you have a green tank against a green background it's hard to spot using just optics, but in TI it stands out as a heat source. We can choose either "white hot" or "black hot" (white being the preferred source) in the sight. Operating by day, you can pick out a target in TI and flick back to optics for a visual ID if necessary. At night we also routinely employ NVGs as an aid

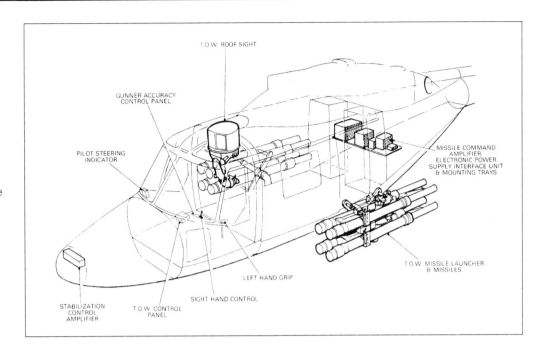

Left: The Westland Lynx AH.7. (Photo: Westland)

Below left: Empty TOW launch tubes, with their guide wire 'boxes'. (Photo: Author)

Right: Lynx TOW install-ation.

Below: A side-on view of the cab-mounted optics for the TOW sighting system. (Photo: Author)

to getting us into the target area, leaving the TI to pick out any potential threats.

'Lynx/TOW carries eight missiles, four on each side of the cab. Fired individually, TOW's maximum range is 3,750m, minimum range 500m. Time of flight to 2,000m is eight seconds, and it is an excellent piece of kit, and very easy to use. From the left-hand seat the air gunner has access to the roof-mounted optics by virtue of a "pull down" monocular sight. At his right hand is a control stick for

lining up and moving the sight's cross-hairs, and at his left hand are the fire buttons plus all the switchology associated with the optics, such as the normal/TI image, focus and magnification controls.

'We carry two versions of the very effective TOW missile, I-TOW (Improved TOW) and FI-TOW (Further Improved TOW). I-TOW will kill any vehicle except main battle tanks from the front. FI-TOW will kill anything from any direction, as it overflies the target and fires its charge downwards, vertically hitting the most vulnerable part of the vehicle. The Lynx/TOW is able to accept any mix of these missiles, and we have a standard loading of four I-TOW on the bottom stations and four FI-TOW on the top stations. A typical engagement with TOW is from the hover, although we did fire on the move during the Gulf War. Speeds varied, but generally it was 30kts. Two modes of "fire" are available to us, "Manual", which means selecting each missile, or "Auto", which means the system selects the next missile to fire. In normal operations we use the latter, as it saves having to "come out of the sight", which is much preferable, especially at night.'

The two Lynx/TOW fly swiftly to the FRV point, hopping over treelines, keeping as low as possible,

BATTLE CATS

Right: All that would be visible to an enemy during an attack would be the rotors and the top of the TOW sight. The air gunner scans for his target, then fixes the cross-hairs firmly on the victim. (Photo: Author)

Below: At the FARP the crews might not have the luxury of a fuel bowser. (Photo: Author)

and having a watchful eye for ground obstructions and, most importantly, any 'wires'. Flying in combat speed, switching positions to cover each other, the Lynx RV with the Gazelle and receive an updated intel report. The crews conduct their FRV drills, switching off any tell-tale active systems, and make their TOW checks. They then 'creep' forward to the battle position as low as they can possibly make it to avoid detection, lifting just enough to clear any obstructions and immediately diving again for cover. Now secured at the BP, 50m back from a treeline, they run through their final checks. The Lynx helicopters then 'lift' a mere 1m above the trees, so all that is visible is their rotors and the all-important TOW sight.

During this 'pop-up' the pilot 'pedals' the Lynx on to the attack heading and the AG acquires his target with the sight set at 2x mag. The crews have already briefed that the Lynx on the left will take all targets on that side and that on the right will look after that area. The AG places his target in the circle that appears at 2x mag. He then flicks to high mag. Everything from the low-mag circle now appears with cross-hairs covering it. He puts the cross-hairs firmly on the designated target and identifies it as hostile.

'Target identified—come in to constraints,' calls McHale. On the right-hand console the pilot checks his TOW sighting unit, which is a manual read-out with its own cross-hairs matched to where the TOW sight is looking. He pedals the aircraft round so that the TSU is looking in the correct direction.

Above: A different perspective on the Lynx in its firing position. The aircraft remains hidden behind the trees during launch, the TOW flying upwards before settling on a horizontal trajectory to the target. (Photo: Author)

Below: Front-line Lynx. Unlike the training versions to be found with No 671 Squadron, this particular Lynx contains all the updates of a battle-ready aircraft. (Photo: Author)

No 671 Squadron AAC

Otherwise known as the Operational Training Squadron, No 671 deals with graduate airmen training on the Lynx and Gazelle helicopters. The unit also runs refresher courses, an aircraft commander's course and continuation training for all Army Air Corps staff pilots at Middle Wallop from the commandant down.

'In constraints,' calls Terrett. In the AG's TOW sight a 'Ready' flag appears, announcing that the correct position has been achieved to fire a missile.

'Mass to TOW,' calls Terrett as the AG sets the missile switch on the main panel. 'Three Blacks.'

'Ready to fire,' is the response.

'3 . . . 2 . . . 1 . . . fire!'

'Firing *now!*' calls the AG as he squeezes the trigger.

'Fire flag,' calls Terrett.

As soon as the trigger is operated a 'fire flag' appears in the AG's sight. This tells him that an electronic signal has been sent to the selected missile. This command winds up the missile's gyros and batteries. One and a half seconds later, the TOW is launched with a brief burst of flame.

The AG keeps the cross-hairs firmly on the target, and, even when launched at maximum range, the TOW is guaranteed to hit the target within two feet of the mark.

Below left: WO2 John McHale uses his 'pull down' TOW sight, selecting his optics, either normal or thermal, to suit conditions. (Photo: Author)

Below right: At his left hand the air gunner has the controls to focus his sight and select the magnification, as well as the trigger to launch the missiles under his crooked index finger. (Photo: Author)

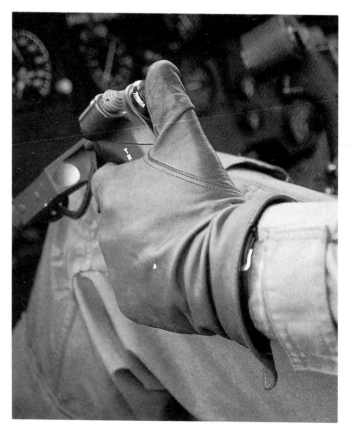

Westland Lynx AH.7

The first flight of the Westland Lynx was made in March 1971, but the helicopter did not see operational service with the Army until 1977, when it emerged as the Lynx AH.1. The current Lynx/TOW aircraft is designated AH.7, which introduced new engines with infra-red suppressors, tail rotor changes, BERP blades, a 'dustbin' IR jammer mounted on the underside of the rear fuselage near the tail boom and external diode formation lights that are compatible with NVGs. The introduction of GPS has also greatly aided navigation. No 671 Squadron use the AH.7 in the training role. Their aircraft have not been blessed with all the 'front-line' additions, but they remain very effective helicopters. (Photo: Westland)

'Impact!' calls the AG.

'Check wires clear,' calls Terrett. The missile's guide wire is automatically cut, but the crew check that they are clear of it before moving. Peter Terrett drops the Lynx back behind the covering trees, and the pair move off to another firing position.

Right: The well-presented interior of the 'operational' Lynx AH.7. (Photo: Author)

Below: An example of a Gazelle AH.1 scout, as used by the aviation reconnaissance patrols. (Photo: Author)

WORLDWIDE COLOUR TV

'Your only safety lies across the Saudi Arabian border. That is where the bombing and starvation stop. The Joint Forces offer you asylum. They offer you a warm bed, medical attention and three filling meals a day. Embrace your Arab brothers and share in their peace'—an extract taken from the 'Voice of the Gulf', broadcast to Iraqi troops on 11 February 1991 from an orbiting EC-130E Hercules of the 193rd Special Operations Group, Pennsylvania Air National Guard, during the Gulf War.

Flown by men whom many call 'The Quiet Professionals', the airborne mission of the 193rd SOG remains shrouded behind a thick veil of secrecy—as do the lives of the men themselves, who are camera-shy to a fault. Flying highly specialized EC-130 aircraft, under the aegis of the Commando Solo (formerly Volant Solo) mission, the unit has as its primary aim the broadcasting of tactical psychological messages using radio and standard television frequencies.

'The aircraft is essentially a flying radio and TV station,' advises Captain Kris Kollar of the 193rd.

Below: Cranking up the undercarriage, the 193rd SOG heads out for another broadcasting sortie. The massive podded antennae and tail fairings make for a very unusual array of appendages on such a large bird. (Photo: Lockheed)

Right, upper: A view of the original Rivet Rider configuration with the large dorsal blade antennae and 'axe-head' wing aerials. (Photo: Knowles)

Right, lower: An EC-130 rolls in behind a tanker to take on gas. As on most long-duration flights, relief crews are carried, and the aircraft can continue its mission without overstressing its airmen. (Photo: Knowles)

Psyops with the Penny ANG's EC-130s

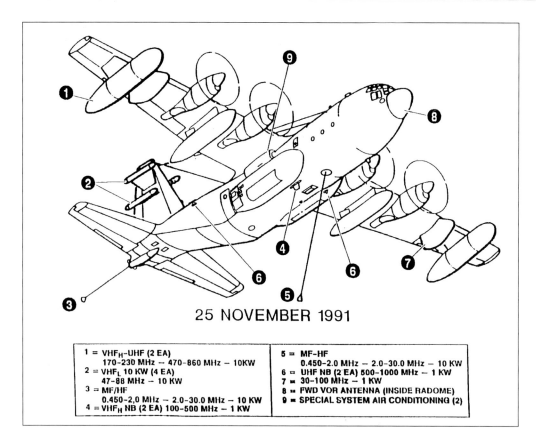

25 NOVEMBER 1991

1 = VHF$_H$-UHF (2 EA)	5 = MF-HF
170-230 MHz — 470-860 MHz — 10KW	0.450-2.0 MHz — 2.0-30.0 MHz — 10 KW
2 = VHF$_L$ 10 KW (4 EA)	6 = UHF NB (2 EA) 500-1000 MHz — 1 KW
47-88 MHz — 10 KW	7 = 30-100 MHz — 1 KW
3 = MF/HF	8 = FWD VOR ANTENNA (INSIDE RADOME)
0.450-2,0 MHz — 2.0-30.0 MHz — 10 KW	9 = SPECIAL SYSTEM AIR CONDITIONING (2)
4 = VHF$_H$ NB (2 EA) 100-500 MHz — 1 KW	

Left: Rivet Rider WWCTV antenna pod status. (USAF)

Below: The busy communications 'cell' inside the EC-130, with tape decks and broadcast systems that would bring a jealous glance from many a small terrestrial TV station! (193 SOG)

Below right: 'The Quiet Professionals' depart on another sortie. (Photo: Lockheed)

'The system is equipped with high-power transmitters, "numerous" antennae and a variety of audio and videotape decks that provide the programme sources. We are able to broadcast over AM/FM radio, short-wave and military communication bands.'

The 'one of a kind' psyop mission is run under the umbrella of the Air National Guard, but when mobilized the 193rd report directly to the Air Forces Special Operations Command. 'Our motto is "Electrons not Bullets",' continues Kris Kollar, 'and we are proud that our brand of hardware can "persuade" the enemy into surrender, not bloodshed, as we were able to do in the Gulf.'

The 193rd operate two types of EC-130. The EC-130E Rivet Rider and the Improved EC-130E(RR) —which latter has only recently been introduced into service—share Harrisburg IAP with the EC-130(CL) Comfy Levi, a highly specialized snooper which performs classified 'Senior Scout' missions.

The original EC-130E(RR), four of which were converted from EC-130(CL)s, were tasked to provide audio and black-and-white TV relay and transmissions. The first EC-130(RR) type, delivered in 1977, has two prominent 'axe-head' anten-

nae at the base of the tail fin. Further antennae are mounted in missile-like canisters located under the wings between the engines.

In 1992 the first of the 'next-generation' Rivet Riders was delivered to the 193rd. Developed by Lockheed Ontario and Rockwell Collins, it has extended the already impressive capabilities of the aircraft, allowing the broadcast of colour television.

Modifications on the new EC-130s include the addition of two 6ft diameter, 23ft long pods mounted under each wing (outboard of the axe-head antennae), and these house the aerials for high-frequency colour TV channels. Also prominent are four 'bullet' fairings protruding from either side of the tail. These are dedicated to low-frequency TV broadcasting, the tail-mounted blade antennae being deleted. Two trailing-wire aerials can be extended, to provide both HF and AM omnidirectional coverage. One is released from a 'beaver tail' at the base of the fin and a second extends from a fairing beneath the fuselage, and this particular 'trailer' is held in position by a 500lb weight. Trans-

mitter power has also been boosted from 1kW to 10kW, substantially increasing the signal range. Self-protection is also enhanced, with the addition of IR jammers and chaff and flare dispensers.

It was on Thanksgiving Day in 1990 that the 193rd began transmitting the 'Voice of the Gulf' into the Kuwait Theatre of Operations, helping to prepare psychologically the battlefield, offering the Iraqi troops food, medicine and rest if they surrendered and leaving them in no doubt of the consequences if they continued to fight. Three EC-130s operated from Riyadh and Abu Dhabi Air Bases and in the process of their psyops operations delivered a record USAF sortie of 21 hours.

'During "Desert Storm" we broadcast prayers from the Koran and messages from captured, well-treated Iraqi prisoners. Soldiers told our intelligence people that they first learned of surrendering through the broadcasts of the 193rd and by reading leaflets dropped by other units. I suppose you could say our mission includes targets that don't usually answer back!

The 193rd Special Operations Group

The history of the 193rd and the development of their Commando Solo mission can be traced back to the Cuban Missile Crisis of 1962, when psyops first became a military requirement. The need for a quick-reacting airborne transmitter became apparent during the Dominican Crisis of 1965, when US troops were frustrated by a rebel-held radio station continually broadcasting delaying tactics to the resistance forces. As a result, approval was given to install some 'off-the-shelf' broadcasting equipment aboard a Lockheed Constellation, which thereby became the EC-121, an aircraft which the 193rd continued to use until the advent of the Hercules in 1977. The Commando Solo technique has been battle-tested so far on four occasions—Operations 'Commando Buzz' (Cambodia, 1970), 'Urgent Fury' (Grenada, 1983), 'Just Cause' (Panama, 1989) and 'Desert Shield'/'Desert Storm' in 1990/91—and at the time of writing the 193rd is involved in the crisis in Haiti. The unit's mission has undergone several name-changes down the years, from 'Coronet Solo' in 1968, through 'Volant Solo' to its current 'Commando Solo' designation.

'Missions begin when a problem area is identified and the appropriate method of psyops decided upon. This process starts at the State Department with a Situation Evaluation. Relevant messages are then produced at the Army's 4th Psychological Operations Group at Fort Bragg. Once the tapes are approved they are delivered to us here at the 193rd. Normally the Joint Forces Commander will form a Joint Psyops Task Force to conduct operations and assign target areas.'

Carrying a crew of twelve, five officers (pilot, co-pilot, navigator, control chief and electronic warfare officer) and seven enlisted men (flight engineer, loadmaster and five mission specialists, who

Above: The bullet fairings on the tail of the EC-130 can be clearly seen in this view, as can the suitability of the grey colour scheme to such a large beast. (Photo: Gensler)

Left: Sunset over Harrisburg IAP. (Photo: 193 SOG)

may also include a linguist seconded from the Army or friendly nations), the EC-130 will ply its trade close to the front lines, usually being covered by AWACS and fighter escorts.

'Once airborne, the mission is co-ordinated by the five electronic communication system operators and the mission control chief. They are situated in the mission compartment, which is located in the main body of the aircraft. These operators occupy either "search" positions, covering medium, high, very high or ultra-high frequencies, or "audio" positions. The mission compartment has cassette and reel-to-reel tape recorders, transmitters and a "live" microphone. The mission control chief plans where the EC-130 will orbit in order to hit the target audience with the best possible signal. We are able to overpower enemy transmissions or broadcast on open frequencies. The search operator also monitors the radio and TV frequencies to find one that is clear of other broadcasts and is within the target area.

'Depending on the frequency, we'll select either HF/MF or VHF/UHF, and the operators tune up their transmitters inside the aircraft, matching them with the corresponding antennae outside. The signals can then be sent from either side of the aircraft, depending on which direction the target is. One of the operators then selects and plays a message across to the transmitting operators, who broadcast its content over the airways. We also rely on other units to aid our cause by dropping leaflets to inform our "audience" of our broadcast frequencies.

'In the Haiti crisis, our objective is to create a creditable and entertaining format that is pro-democracy and pro-Aristide, with messages interspersed with news, discussions and pop music, giving the Haitians hope that things will get better. Slowly orbiting off Western Haiti, messages are also broadcast in Creole, the language of the majority of the islanders.

'As you can see, messages are prepared in the native tongue of the target audience and crews are not always able to understand what is being said;

Right: Despite its many appendages the EC-130 still has a very commendable performance, although the greater drag from the external pods is a problem. (Photo: 193 SOG)

Below: A 'Penny ANG' EC-130 Rivet Rider prepares for another day with its brand of psyops. The aircraft displays its prominent fairings on the tail, giving it the means to broadcast 'worldwide colour TV'. (Photo: 193 SOG)

Below right: EC-130 on the Harrisburg Ramp. (Photo: 193 SOG)

however, we are always confident that what is broadcast is factual and correct. One thing that is important is that we may not see the results of our psyops until months later, but we know that our actions make a significant difference, not only in wartime but also in peacetime emergency situations.'

Training for Psyops

Training the crews for the EC-130E is an intensive and comprehensive business. All air crew personnel attend a one-week psychological operations course at the Special Operations School at Hurlburt Field. Mission control chiefs are already experienced navigators, and along with the EWOs they attend a 90-day programme where they learn how to operate and to employ to the best advantage the aircraft's complex systems. Enlisted crew are trained for 42 weeks at Keesler AFB, where they learn about ground and airborne radio transmitters. They return to the 193rd for a unique 180-day upgrade programme, and their total training period lasts for more than two and a half years. Air crews are tasked to fly some 48 training periods in a year in order to remain current, and most sorties are carried out over the sea, where the specialized brand of radio and TV is less likely to be overheard. These sorties each last an average of two or three hours.

HOG HEAVEN

'I am probably very prejudiced about my aircraft, but I firmly believe that the Warthog is the most formidable fighting machine there is for the CAS, SARCAP, FAC and night mission'— confident claims by Lieutenant Alan 'Boots' Vinson, a 'Hog Driver' with the 47th Fighter Squadron, AFRES, flying out of Barksdale AFB in Louisiana.

'It's the ugliest aircraft imaginable, but it's the most survivable one in the inventory. Armour-plated cockpit, interchangeable engines (we can recover with just one "fan" still turning), twin tails, and back-up systems that back-up the back-ups! Its superior loiter capability lends well to the multiple missions we fly at Barksdale, and as a FAC platform (some aircraft carry the OA-10 designation— "O" for Observation) its excellent cockpit visibility and abundance of radios (UHF, VHF and FM) allow the pilot to co-ordinate with outside agencies whilst controlling strike frequencies.

'In the CAS role we are unmatched for a jet, with perhaps only the Harrier coming close, but then they don't possess "The Gun". This is our fearsome GAU-8/A Avenger cannon, its 30mm calibre and seven rotary barrels that spew out milk bottle-sized, high-explosive, armour-piercing rounds, ideal against tanks and vehicles and pretty useful in other areas as well! Eleven stores pylons enable us to carry most weaponry available in the US, with Mavericks, LGBs and CBUs being our "popular choice".

'We are currently putting some of our pilots through SARCAP training (search and rescue combat air patrol), or "Sandy", which will enable us to escort the Jolly Greens to rescue downed airmen in hostile environments. Although some regard the Hog as being very slow, this is one of our strengths. Spotting targets, as opposed to designating targets, is crucial in the CAS business, and we are able to employ our Mavericks at greater stand-off ranges than the "fast-movers" because we have such a short turn radius and more time: we can pop, launch and re-mask without ever having to enter the threat ring. NVGs are also becoming part of our lives, and we have formed an NVG cadre. Our

Below: Caught racing down the runway, a former Alconbury resident pushes the power on to its rotate speed. (Photo: Smith)

47th Fighter Squadron

Established in 1940 as the 47th Pursuit Squadron, the unit spent its first four years in Hawaii as part of the 15th Fighter Group, flying the P-40. Late in 1945 it was shipped to Iwo Jima and on landing began flying close-support missions for the Marines. After the war the 47th was assigned a variety of locations, missions and aircraft. During the 1950s it flew the F-86 and F-102 based at Niagara Falls and during the 1960s operated the F-84 and F-4 at McDill and Ubon, before eventual deactivation and transfer to the Air Force Reserve in 1970. This move was not seen as a death knell but as a rekindling of the 'Old 47th Spirit', and the unit became involved with the A-37 in 1973 at Barksdale, converting to the A-10 in 1980 as part of the 917th Fighter Group, then Tactical Fighter Wing, and finally Fighter Wing. The Squadron patch shows the 'Tarnip Termite', once described as so terrible that even Superman would flinch under its attack! Since the arrival of the A-10 the unit has been involved solely in the ground attack role, although it has now taken on forward air control and search and rescue combat air patrol, with a number of the Hogs designated OA-10s ('O' for Observation) to reflect the new mission status.

cockpit lighting is being modified to suit the use of the goggles.'

Since the Gulf War the A-10 has seen something of a revival in its fortunes, due in no small way to its success on the battlefield, and a number of updates are on the way. LASTE (Low Altitude Safety and Targeting Enhancement) as well as ATHS (Automatic Target Handoff System) have been fitted to several aircraft, and further modifications, such as FLIR and wide-angle HUD, are on the horizon.

'The Hog's cockpit is pretty comprehensive now. On the left console are the radios, emergency flight controls, fuel cut-off, IFF, SAS (Stability Augmentation System) and LASTE panels. The centre section houses the basic flight and engine instruments, HUD controls (which power up the LASTE computer), RWR scope/controls, TV monitor and Pave Penny controls. Along the right are the INS, ECM and electrical panels, environmental controls, lighting, ILS, TACAN chaff/flares and the HARS (Heading Attitude Reference System).'

'The UHF radio has "Have Quick", a programme that is jam-resistant, using a handful of differing frequencies and a specific skip pattern. There is a secure-voice scrambler, so we can scramble our skipping UHF too. SAS provides auto turn co-ordination and dampens the oscillation in both yaw and pitch axes at high speed. It is also the medium through which the LASTE's low-altitude autopilot works.

'LASTE has really revolutionized the Hog and the mod should really have led to the aircraft being

Below: The business end of the A-10: a close-up of the highly polished barrel of the Avenger cannon. (Photo: Author)

Lt Alan Vinson
Lt Alan 'Boots' Vinson is a 25-year-old pilot with the 47th Fighter Squadron, United States Air Force Reserve, and is in his second year with the unit at Barksdale AFB, where he is also one of the Squadron's two schedulers. (Photo: 47 FS)

Lt Alan Vinson
Lt Alan 'Boots' Vinson is a 25-year-old pilot with the 47th Fighter Squadron, United States Air Force Reserve, and is in his second year with the unit at Barksdale AFB, where he is also one of the Squadron's two schedulers. (Photo: 47 FS)

Right: A trail of A-10s under the 'AFRES Aerials' banner. (Photo: 917 FW)

a projected bomb impact line and CCIP. The CCIP, with precision altitude control, activated by the trigger, has also increased the effective range of the GAU-8. The pilot can now select gun cross-hairs for reference or a "pipper" which has a reticle with range bar. Version 4.0 has also "incorporated range information" for the Mavericks via a symbol in the HUD. The system provides an automatic "up vector" when the gun is fired, counteracting the Hog's tendency to dip its snout when the trigger is pulled.

'LASTE has also brought "Bitchin' Betty" into the cockpit, and her electronic voice warns us if we descend below a set altitude (AGL or MSL). She calls "Altitude . . . altitude! Pull up, pull up!" if she calculates we're gonna hit terra firma if a max performance recovery isn't initiated now. She also tells us that the speed brakes are open if we select max power with the "boards" still hangin' out.

'Unless we're a FAC mission, you'll never catch us single-ship. Flight Lead is responsible for the nav, and getting us into the target area; No 2 is responsible for position, clearing the flight and backing up Lead's navigation. Sometimes we'll go four-ship, and in that case Lead has the same job, but now he has three further back-ups, and more eyes checking the "six".

'A flight begins with an intel brief on the scenario, threats, targets and friendliness. The Supervisor of Flying ensures that everyone gets a take-off/landing data sheet (TOLD), weather and any special instructions (SPINS). Lead may delegate portions of the brief, but he will overview the tactics, knowing that these could change en route or at target. (Our call-signs at the 47th are always "Swine".) This usually takes an hour and a quarter. We'll then step out, sign for the jets, which for an anti-armour strike will have a full load of 30mm ammo, (1,174 rounds) in combat mix, containing API (armour-piercing incendiary)—this is the strong stuff, with a depleted uranium core which punches

redesignated the A-10B: it's made that much difference, especially the 4.0 version. LASTE has dramatically increased the combat effectiveness of an already powerful aircraft. Essentially LASTE takes out the guesswork of bomb theory, and with CCIP (constantly computed impact point) all we have to worry about is our abort altitude. LASTE uses the dive angle taken from the INS and pilot-entered target elevation and altitude (radar, baro or delta) to compute the slant range. Using that, plus a ballistics table for the weapon selected, it produces

Above left: The Barksdale tail-code. (Photo: 917 FW)

Above centre: Barksdale nose marking and Pave Penny designator. (Photo: 917 FW)

Above: The high-placed canopy of the A-10 affords the pilot excellent visibility, and this, together with its loiter time and ability to tote a huge range of weaponry, makes the aircraft an ideal choice for the FAC role. (Photo: Author)

holes straight through armour plate—and standard HEI (high-explosive incendiary). The gun has a dual feed system, one feed for each type, and theoretically with both feeds "in" we could fire off 4,200rpms [rounds per minute].

'We'll have at least four Mavericks (two TV and two IR) and between four and six cans of Rockeye CBU on board. Walkround is standard. However, I am always concerned with the explosives hangin' on the jet, so I check the pins, fuses and ejectors carefully. Settling into the "office", I connect the clips on my harness and LPU, zip up my G-suit and crank it down tighter over my legs, check the seat kit, belt, and adjust the rudder pedals while the

HOG HEAVEN

Right: Silhouetted against the bright clouds, a Barksdale Hog demonstrates its 'ugly' characteristics. (Photo: Author)

Far right: Loaded with twin 'Winders, Maverick missiles and ECM pod, an A-10 awaits its turn to 'gas-up'. (Photo: via Perron)

Below right: Plugging into an Air Force tanker. The Hog is unique in having its IFR receptacle in its 'snout'. (Photo: 917 FW)

Below far right: Another view showing the A-10's high-placed canopy. (Photo: Author)

crew chief grabs the harness connectors. I hold open the releases and give 'em a tug after he hooks me in. I strap on my knee boards and don the "noodle protector", oxygen hose and comm cord.

'I punch up the battery inverter, dial in the ATIS, check the intercom with the chief, check the fire circuits and crank up the APU, align the INS and turn on the electronic gizmos and let them run their BIT checks. Lead calls up on the three radios, Have Quick and secure-voice. We go to ground freq' and crank up the engine.

'The Hog cranks up real easy. Check the starter valve is normal, ITT below 100 degrees, bring the throttle over the "hump" to idle, hack the clock and watch. The "Eng Start Cycle" lights up, core RPM comes alive and oil and fuel both "light off" at ten seconds. A rumble to the rear, and the fans of the TF-34s come to life. Through 40 per cent the hydraulics pressurize, the stick flinches in response to 3,000psi, at 52 per cent the generator comes on line and at 56 per cent we take a ten-second count for the "cycle" light to go out and the APU to unload. After a series of control checks—flaps, speed brakes, SAS and trim—the chief gives the bird a last look and disconnects the comm cord.

"Swine check . . . 1 . . . 2."

'I give the chief the "Pull chocks" signal, stand on the brakes and get set to taxi. Moving out, I get the maps ready and look for any final LASTE or INS updates. I carefully review the line-up card, keep-

ing a sharp look-out across the pan—believe me, these pilot jobs are hard to come by and I don't want to be the guy who bumps into the dude on the runway sweeper truck! I pull into the "last chance" arming area and get my hands into view, confirming on my comm that the configuration in the windows of my armament control panel matches the bits hangin' on the wings. Switches safe and

normal, hot gun, all armed up, strobes on, and ALR-69 RWR on. Lead signals the tower we are ready to go.

"'Swine check . . . 1 . . . 2.'"

'Taxi into position. I review the TOLD, heat, seat, skid, squawk, SAS and flaps, run up the engines and switch to departure control. Take-off is at 20-second intervals, brakes off, max power! Check speed at 1,000 feet, predicted fan speed, runway remaining, go/no-go. Rotate comes up and I engage a positive climb out, pulling in the gear and flaps.

'We take a high-level ingress to the AO (area of operations) and departure control hands us off to AWACS. After authentication we pass our line up and get any updates. They hand us off to an ABCCC (Airborne Command and Control Center), who will

Above: Lead 'pulls off; now reverse roles. Lead will suppress with the gun; No 2 will drop CBUs in ripple within five seconds of Lead's strafe run, taking advantage of the gun's ability to keep heads down.' (Gavin McLeod)

deal with the specifics of our mission. Finally, we check in with our FAC.

'We plan to hit the target with CBU first, but if it proves to be "hot" we'll use Mavericks at a stand-off range and hose them down with a few 30mm rounds before laying down the canisters.

'Because of our loiter time (two hours fully "bombed up"), we tote a boat-load of chaff and flares

(480 bundles), carried in batteries of AN/ALE-40 dispensers, and we are able to mount a number of external jammer pods such as the ALQ-131. The FAC is invaluable to the CAS role. He sees what the fighters see, and knows the ground commander's objectives. He passes us the "nine-line brief", and we then hold our own fighter-to-fighter brief. The target is "hot" so we plan "Wedge", "Shooter", "Cover" and "Maverick". Formation timing is "Wedge", Lead will be "Shooter", No 2 will be "Cover" and monitor Lead's heads down time with "Maverick". "Swine 1" (Lead) gets an early target and calls up the video. He then uses the HUD's symbology to place his Maverick's seeker head on target. Space-stabilize the seeker in a fixed position, check the TVM for a good lock, consent lock . . . fire!

'He pulls off; now reverse roles. Lead will suppress with the gun; No 2 will drop CBUs in ripple within five seconds of Lead's strafe run, taking advantage of the gun's ability to keep heads down. We are, however, susceptible to ground fire in a bomb run. You can't jink successfully and keep a bead on the target, so Lead comes in at the 90-degree to target and rakes off a ten-second burst, fish-tailing the aircraft with the rudder to get a good spread. The Hog is able to take small-arms hits—we have a titanium bath-tub protecting the

Left: The scene on the Basra Road during the Gulf War following the 'turkey shoot' by Allied warplanes which included attacks by A-10s. (Photo: via Tomlinson)

pilot, plus the flight controls are duplicated and spaced out, so if we take a hit we can still manoeuvre. The fuel tanks are self-sealing, and even if the "mains" are ripped open we can still fly 370km on the contents of small sump tanks.

'The Avenger gun is very versatile, and there are not many targets it cannot be employed against: even air-to-air is now possible with the LASTE sight, but still the most common employment is "point and shoot". This thing is 22 feet long and can fire 70 rounds per second, and a 100-round burst can take 5 knots off your airspeed—*thud*—like hitting a wall. Using LASTE and the Maverick, we can now fire the gun at night with the same accuracy as in daylight, using a "grapefruit strafe". First the pilot locks up the target with a Maverick, then he moves the aircraft so as to overlay the gun cross-hairs into the "grapefruit" shaped symbol of the missile. LASTE corrects the wind and bullet drop, and as the gun fires you can see the rounds tracking downward through the TVM.

'The FAC could use a MULE to lase a target, and assist acquisition. Our Pave Penny will pick up the reflection and display a diamond in the HUD, telling us where the target is and informing the Mavericks where to "look". The Pave Penny pod is suspended beneath the forward fuselage on a pylon, and it locates and tracks targets designated by ground or airborne lasers. We listen up to the FAC's assessments and we can continue to attack until our CBUs, Mavericks or shells are "Winchester" [out], or we hit bingo fuel. Pull off target and then return to base, after getting a BDA from the FAC and passing an IFREP (in-flight report) to our controlling agency. Back at base we'll debrief, either in the building or, if it's an ICT turnaround, whilst we are in the jets getting reloaded.

'The Hog's a mean machine. It ain't fast, it ain't stylish, but don't mess with us—ugly but well-hung!'

Below left: When based at RAF Alconbury, this A-10 chalked up a number of 'kills' during its stint in the Gulf War. For a brief period of time the unit were happy to advertise their skills. (Photo: Author)

Below right: The A-10's large number of pylons allow it to carry a huge variety of ordnance on one mission. Here we see just a taste, with rocket pod and Maverick missiles adorning this example. The updates to the Hog have meant a huge step forward in operations, especially using the Maverick. (Photo: Author)

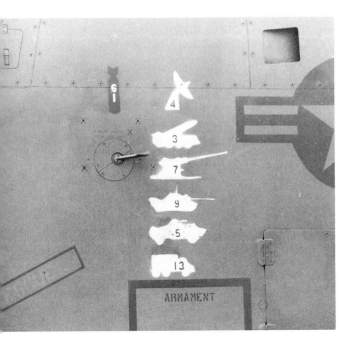

TANKING WITH THE NIGHT OWLS

The success of many of the missions undertaken by the US Air Forces Special Operations Command depends on the ability to extend the range or loiter time of its helicopter forces. By definition, a mission brief will see them operating in sensitive areas or behind enemy lines, and these clandestine operations call for a specialized type of airborne tanker. To fulfil this need, once again a modified version of the ubiquitous Hercules has been brought into service—the HC-130N/P Combat Shadow.

'Our primary mission is the aerial refuelling of Pave Low helicopters, and we can provide them with a single or multi-ship mission dependent on the number of helos to be gassed up,' explains Captain Roger Williams, a Combat Shadow Pilot from the 67th Special Operations Squadron, based at RAF Alconbury in England and part of the 352nd SOG, United States Air Forces Europe. 'We fly at low level, in or near hostile territory, and mostly under the cover of darkness. We have secondary roles roughly similar to the MC-130—air-dropping small special teams, small cargo loads, rubber raiding craft and Zodiac boats—but the MC guys can do it better because they have the high-tech systems geared up to that type of work.

'Compared to the MC-130 and all their wizardry, there is only one word to describe our systems—

Above: The HC-130 has the designation 'Combat Shadow', a name that seems to fit this photograph very neatly as one of the 'Night Owls' is silhouetted against an almost golden ocean. (Photo: 67 SOS)

Left: The Combat Shadow Hercules based at Alconbury have two distinctive nose shapes, the 'Fulton nose', seen here, and the standard 'Pinocchio nose'. (Photo: Mark Smith)

HC-130N/P Combat Shadow

primitive! Currently we have little in the way of "high tech": basically we are totally visual! Considering our mission calls for us to fly low-level, we do not possess any sort of terrain-avoidance radar (T/A) . . . Well, that's not strictly true. Our T/A sits looking out of the window wearing a pair of NVGs, hoping to spot the ground. We call it the navigator!'

The HC-130 was originally ordered in 1963, and it first flew in 1964. It has subsequently served in many roles and missions. In Vietnam the type was used to refuel the Jolly and Super Jolly Green Giant helicopters, and also as an airborne command and control platform, to direct, and later to conduct, combat search and rescue efforts. Four of their number were also modified to launch remotely

piloted vehicles (RPV). The HC-130 is easily recognized by its unmistakable dorsal 'hump' containing the unique AN/ARD-17 'Cook Tracker' receivers—originally designed to plot returning space capsules but found to be of greater use in the CSAR role picking up faint signals from below—and some aircraft also have the Fulton Recovery System nose modification. Another distinguishing feature is the low-mounted window each side of the fuselage, in front of the wheel bays. These are again for use in the CSAR role, crew members being seated in 'search' positions in the main cargo area, and on the starboard search station are the controls for the AN/ARD-17 system. The aircraft have two trailing-hose refuelling pods on their outer wing hardpoints,

TANKING WITH THE NIGHT OWLS

Combat Shadow Crew
Captain Roger Williams Jr (left) trained on the HC-130 at Kirtland AFB after undergoing basic flight training on the T-37. Captain Brian Yates (centre) came to the HC-130 directly out of Navigator School. MSgt Rick Wells (right) is a loadmaster who cross-trained to aircrew from the Security Police. He learned his trade on the MC-130 at Pope AFB and has since served at Kadena, Woodbridge and Alconbury with the aircraft.

Above: The standard 'Pinocchio nose' of the Combat Shadow. Despite its nocturnal low-level mission, the aircraft does not feature any of the high-tech systems bestowed on the MC-130. 'Primitive' is the word used to describe its avionics. (Photo: Author)

Below: Left over from the aircraft's combat search and rescue days are the low-mounted windows on either side of the fuselage. (Photo: Author)

Below right: The cockpit of the HC-130 Hercules is austere in comparison to that of the MC-130, but the aircraft nevertheless flies a low-level mission. There is no TF/TA radar, and crews joke that their terrain-following system sits at the window wearing NVGs—he's called the navigator! (Photo: Author)

and self defence is provided by copious numbers of chaff and flare dispensers fitted to the rear fuselage and to the rear of the inner wing pylons. The upper portion of the cargo ramp has also been modified to carry high-power flares for illuminating drop sites at night. The aircraft carries a crew of eight, comprising four officers (pilot, co-pilot, primary navigator and secondary navigator) and four enlisted men

(communications systems operator, flight engineer and two loadmasters).

'Here in the UK we work hand in hand with the 21st SOS,' continues Roger Williams. 'Basically, where they're at, so are we. We pride ourselves in being there for them, as it would be a bad day for us if they ran out of gas and had to walk home! Our tanking operations with the 21st can take place at

Above: Tanking close to the whirling blades of such a large helicopter as the Pave Low is demanding at the best of times, but at heights of 100ft it requires consummate skill by both parties. (Photo: Mark Smith)

Below left: One of a possible two 11,000lb 'Benson' tanks fitted in the mid-section of the cargo area. (Photo: Author)

Below: Above the 'Benson' tanks can be found a variety of rescue equipment, such as liferafts. (Photo: Author)

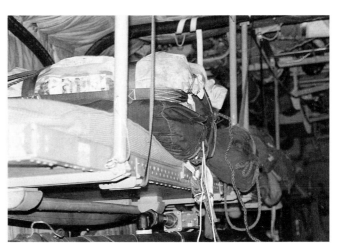

Above: Atop the fuselage is the unusual radome for the AN/ARD-17 'Cook Tracker'. Originally used to plot re-entering space capsules, the system also proved to be very good at locating faint signals from downed airmen. (Photo: Author)

Above right: A little propeller art, in the form of a 'Shamu'. (Photo: Author)

Below: Through the green world of NVGs, two HC-130s in trail formation hunt for their chicks—a gaggle of MH-53J Pave Low helicopters. Night-time close-formation tanking is the Combat Shadow's speciality: 'Believe me, at night, comm out, this is serious flying!' (Photo: Author)

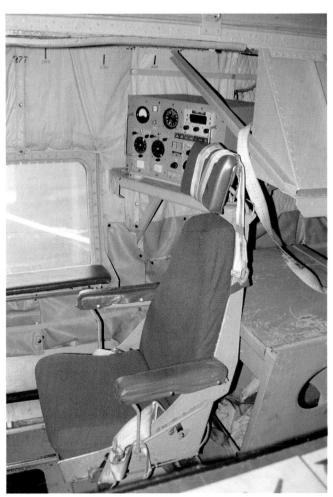

anything between 100 and 1,000ft, comm out, lights out, both internal and external. We currently operate at night using our NVGs. However, we do not as yet have NVG-compatible cockpit lighting—in fact, we have to break chem-sticks in half and tape them to the panels just so we can see the primary flight instruments! Also, unlike the MC-130, we still rely on maps and charts to get us where we're going, hence we have two navs and no computer-aided flight plan. Our reliance on NVGs cannot be em-phasized enough, and we regularly practise NVG-aided landings and take-offs in complete darkness.

'We normally pass fuel at around 115 knots, which is really close to our stall speed, and very slow for such a big airplane. Our normal join-up with the helos means that they like to be on-time/early, whereas we like to be on-time/late at the RV. That gives us time to catch up and overtake them, roll out the hoses and let them plug in. Tactical altitude for refuel is "low". We did get down to 100ft

Above: One of the 67th SOS's tankers gets airborne from Alconbury, this example being fitted with the nose section to mount the Fulton STARS Recovery System. (Photo: Mark Smith)

Left: Situated just behind the flight-deck bulkhead in the main cargo compartment is the right scanner's position, and behind this can be seen the controls for the 'Cook Tracker.' (Photo: Author)

67th Special Operations Squadron
The unit was activated in 1952 as the 67th Air Rescue Squadron, and its primary missions were to attend aircraft accident victims and support Air Force search and rescue efforts. The 67th, by now re-designated the 67th Air Recovery Squadron, moved to Moron AFB in Spain during 1966 in order to bolster the rescue services in that area and was transferred to RAF Woodbridge in 1970. Another name change came about in 1988 when the unit became the 67th Special Operations Squadron, changing roles from rescue to refuelling Special Operations helicopters. Combat Shadows have taken part in such operations as 'Proven Force', 'Provide Comfort' and 'Provide Comfort II', as well as 'Desert Shield' and 'Desert Storm'.

in "Desert Storm" with the hoses out, and that was really wild.

'We sometimes have problems meeting up with the Pave Lows; maybe they're late, or not where they said they would be: in these instances we have a number of "methods" to find them. We can use the TACAN or IFF interrogator, or we can try the C-130's radar, but like other "slick 130s" it's not designed for air intercept. There is always the NVG-aided mark one eyeball, or a technique we call "skin painting", where the nav uses our APN-59 weather radar to "bounce a signal" off them. It's an art, but one that the navs have developed a real flair for. Trying to pick out an MH-53 on their scope is tough, but they can even pick out a Pave Hawk, which is a much smaller aircraft, with some ease!

'We try where possible to tank in as low-threat an environment as we can; this gives all parties the best possible chance of survival. Once we have picked up our Pave Lows, either visually or "skin-painted", we line up about three miles behind them —although we also practise head-on contacts—then the chase is on. One mile out, the flaps are set to 70 per cent and the speed is pegged back to between

115 and 120 knots. As we close, the nav starts calling off the closure, and as we come abeam, the flight engineer rolls out the hoses. On passing our "customers" we ensure we have a good height separation above them and a good visual.

'At the rear the loadmaster now becomes the pilot's eyes, giving him constant updates about the helo's progress as they move into pre-contact positions. Once contact is made, a light comes up on the flight engineer's panel and he begins the fuel transfer. We have two methods of refuelling, 'Automatic',

Left, upper: On the runway at Alconbury, a 67th SOS Combat Shadow tanker returns to its operating centre following an RV with the 21st SOS and their Pave Low helicopters. (Author)

Left, lower: Mounted on the cargo ramp are the launch tubes for ten high-powered flares. (Photo: Author)

Right: Another view of a 'standard' Combat Shadow. (Photo: Author)

Right, lower: A view forward of one of the HC-130's two refuelling pods. (Photo: Author)

which means the engineer dials in a set amount and the feed shuts off at that point, or purely 'Manual' where the Pave Low decides how much he wants to take on board.

'The interphone chatter on board is intense. There is a constant stream of information going to and fro. Because we have so little in the way of systems, we are heavily reliant on verbal comms from all stations. The Pave Lows usually take on around 7,000lb of gas, and we have up to 82,500lb to give away when fully loaded. The fuel is carried within the HC-130's own tanks as well as in up to two 11,000lb "Benson" tanks mounted in the mid-section of the cargo hold.

'Close-formation tanking is another of our specialities. This is when we fly two or more tankers in very close formation if we need to gas up a large number of helicopters. Believe me, at night, comm out, this is serious flying!

'Transloading is another aspect of our operations that we practise with the Pave Lows. If, say, they had picked up a casualty, we could be waiting at a nearby airstrip with our ramp down. They come in and land "back to back" with their ramps down and

transfer the patients to us so we can then make a quick exit.'

An update programme is currently under way to give the HC-130s more in the way of modern equipment, thus making their mission more like that of the MC-130. They will receive a better INS, GPS and NVG-compatible lighting. They will also have a FLIR, RWR and improved chaff and flare dispensers, as well as an IFR capability as a receiver. The future looks bright for the work of the 'Shadow'.

FAST, FLEXIBLE FIREPOWER

'Our objective is to provide fast, flexible firepower and aerial support to the Marine on the ground,' explains Captain John Scott Walsh—call-sign 'Vapour'—of Marine Attack Squadron 542, the 'Tigers' who fly the incomparable AV-8B Harrier II. 'In the CAS role there is no better aircraft, and the Corps' aim is to be a near-total VSTOL force by the late 1990s. The Marine doctrine is that of "manoeuvre warfare", and with the characteristics the Harrier possesses we are not tied to any fixed base and our aircraft can be readily positioned close to the FLOT and FEBA. This gives the "grunts" a much faster reaction time should they need to call in aerial firepower—which of course means we can have bombs on target and suppress enemy defences much faster and with greater efficiency as we are only a few miles from the BZ, rather than a call to a major base or carrier that could be positioned hundreds of miles away.

'Perhaps the easiest way to disable any air force is to put a bomb in the middle of its runways, so the Marines do not want to be tied to large operating bases. We want to be able to deploy from our amphibious assault ships, establish a beach-head and commit to our manoeuvre warfare.

'We are the artillery of the Corps, so when the Marines break from their beach-head and force a breach through enemy positions we can respond to their needs. They could be funnelling through "asshole to belly-button" and be exposed to all kinds

Captain John Scott Walsh
John Scott Walsh is 33 years of age and a graduate of the University of California at Berkeley. His decision to join the Marines was based on the Corps' reputation and the challenge to be one of the 'élite'. During his training as a Marine 2nd Lieutenant he decided to specialize in aviation, and on graduation from Quantico he was posted to Pensacola to train as a flyer. Basic Flight School saw him fly the T-38C, Intermediate School the T-2 and Advanced School the TA-4. On successfully completing his training he was selected to fly the Harrier and was assigned to VMAT-203 at Cherry Point, where he progressed to his current unit, VMA-542. (Photo: Author)

of threats, from rocket-launchers to well dug-in troops. They call for us, the "artillery", because they know we are so close and our response time will be minimal. The Gulf War gave the world a good indication of the Marine operations when Harriers flew direct to the Gulf or deployed from assault ships to a forward operating base at King Khaled International Airport, close to friendly forces.

'The first task before any mission is to study the day's ATO (air tasking order) and see what is required. I see that our primary objective is to attack artillery tubes in Kuwait, with a secondary role of flying "armed alert", to be called in if required by other agencies needing a specific target to be dealt with. Fuel requirements were never a

problem as we were based close to the action, and we also had a FARP (forward arming and refuelling point) located at Tanajib, which was about 30 miles from the Kuwaiti border. We look at the frequencies on our ciphered radios and check the comm plan to see whether we are dealing with a ground or airborne FAC, and also detail our IFF codes.

'The weapon load and settings are then discussed, based on the target, and for this attack 500lb Mk 82 "slick" bombs are the perfect choice. We then look at take-off, RV and formation for the

Below: In the more familiar grey/green camouflage, a Harrier on a training sortie lets go two Mk 82 Snakeye bombs. (Photo: McDonnell Douglas)

outbound leg and look at the attack formation at the target. We discuss battle damage, and what our options are if one of us goes down.

'We turn then to a detailed analysis of our attack, having defined the tubes; and the weapons, "quantity", "multiple" and "interval" are all decided. In this instance, quantity will be six (six 500-pounders carried), "multiple" will be two (two bombs at a time eject when we hit the "pickle" button) and "interval" will be 150ft (spread of the weapon). Fusing is also decided and set.

'The delivery angle and mode is then agreed, (steep-dive, high-airspeed) and we decide whether to use the ARBS/DMT or a CCIP. [The Hughes ABB-19(V) Angle Rate Bombing System/Dual Mode Tracker is the most accurate system in the Marine inventory: as the computer automatically hands off the weapons, this uses a combined laser and TV camera to measure range and slant angle.] Based on the perceived threat, I decide on my expendables (chaff and flares) and look at mutual support and our "calls" for triple-A and "bogeys". Time is then spent on a detailed target study, based on the latest frag and intel. We need to know what the target will look like, how it will appear to us as we roll in, what the sun angle is likely to be and what are the known defences.

'I then collect my flight gear, torso harness and survival vest, which contains water, space blankets, flares and a mirror. I also add a candle, matches, an extra blanket, extra water and some camouflage paint. I strap on my trusty 9mm pistol

Left: Thumbs up! John Walsh ready to launch from the USS *Guam*. (Photo: Author)

Right: The Harriers 'went grey' while on duty in the Gulf, covering their existing grey/green 'wraparound' scheme with a two-tone grey finish. (Photo: Mike Kopack)

Left: At the tip of the AV-8B's nose is the very useful Angle Rate Bombing System and Dual Mode Tracker 'window'. (Photo: Author)

VMFA-542

Marine Aviation Squadron 542 was first commissioned as Marine Night Fighter Squadron 542 at MCAS Cherry Point in 1944, then flying the F6F Hellcat. Following active service during the latter part of the Second World War and during the Korean War, the unit was deactivated in 1970. The arrival of the AV-8A Harrier saw the Squadron re-activated in 1972 at MCAS Beaufort, and it moved back to its original home, Cherry Point, in 1975. In April 1986 the trusty AV-8A and AV-8Cs were retired as the unit acquired new AV-8Bs.

and survival knife, make sure I'm "sanitized" and it's out to the jet.'

For the mission, the Harrier is configured with the six bombs, an ALQ-164 ECM pod on the centreline station and a 25mm cannon and shells. The AV-8B is fitted with a podded General Electric GAU-12 five-barrel cannon known as 'The Equalizer'. The cannon and its pneumatic drive system are located in the port-side pod, with 300 rounds of ammunition in the starboard pod linked by a 'bridge' which carries the rounds across to the gun.

'Walk-round complete, I climb aboard and strap in. The cockpit of my AV-8B is much roomier than the early models, incorporates high-tech multi-function displays and has HOTAS [hands-on-throt-tle-and-stick] capabilities. I put on my kneeboard with target details and frequencies etc. and I wind up the APU to brind the electrics on line. I begin to programme all of the waypoints into the computer, along with the target location, using the UFC (up-front controller). I set the rad-alt to the correct height, oxygen on, lighting set up, fuel feed set, nozzle lever set, flight control systems set. Punch into the armament control panel my weapons, quantity, multiple, delivery and fusing, call up the plan view of the aircraft from the computer on to one of the MFDs and check that what it thinks I am carrying is correct. Check the fuel and set my aural tones, expendables are set and on, my RWR is on line, ECM pod on, radios are on—all okay. I open up

FAST, FLEXIBLE FIREPOWER

the fuel valve and hit the starter. In a couple of seconds the plane roars into life and the Plane Captain goes through pre-flight checks with me, ensuring all of the flying surfaces etc. are free. He hands me off to the Ordnance Captain, who arms the weapons, and in turn it's back to the Plane Captain, who gives me a final look-over before directing me to the runway.

'All set. The computer calculates the rotate speed based on the weight of the aircraft and the temperature. The power is run to full, the rpm races through 55 per cent. Check the acceleration time, jetpipe temperature, set the nozzles, set the flaps to 62 degrees. All looks good, the power goes on, full rpm comes up in the HUD, brakes off . . . and away. Twenty-one thousand pounds of thrust pump the aircraft down the runway, the computer cues the rotate speed . . . 84 . . . 85 knots . . . slap the nozzle lever back and the plane leaps into the air. Gear up, flaps in. A check with my wingman that he is up and okay, and we press forward with the mission.

Above: It's a waiting game until launch time arrives, so it's a good moment to collect your thoughts. (Photo: Author)

Left: A Harrier launches from the USS *Belleau Wood*. (Photo: McDonnell Douglas)

Right, upper: Immediately after the Gulf War, a 'Tigers' Harrier surveys Kuwait's burning oilfields. (Photo: McDonnell Douglas)

Right, lower: Getting a Harrier aboard ship is a tricky business. There are no arrester wires to trap you, so its an aerial ballet to spot the aircraft where you want to be—and a task made more difficult by a rolling deck. (Photo: Author)

FAST, FLEXIBLE FIREPOWER

Left: Ground crews load up the aircraft with fire bombs (napalm) and Rockeye CBUs. (Photo: J. S. Walsh)

Below right: John Walsh runs through his control wipe-out sequence under the watchful eye of the Plane Captain, who ensures that all the flying surfaces are in good order. (Photo: Author)

'After the climb-out I call up the Tactical Air Operations Center and let them know we are airborne, and get a threat update from them. They clear us to a holding point, where I contact the Direct Air Support Center and Fire Control Center They hand us off to a Marine ANGLICO (Air and Naval Gunfire Liaison Company) team who will be handling our mission. The ANGLICO team are located up near the coast, where they have spotted the artillery tubes we are tasked to deal with. DASC moves us out to another holding point, where we obtain direct contact with the ANGLICO guys. They read us a standard "nine-line brief". This gives us an initial point to hold at, heading to target, distance to target, target elevation, target co-ordinates, target description, what kind of mark they are going to put on the target, where the friendly forces are located and our egress direction. They give us a time check—four minutes TOT. We hit our stopwatches and enter the new target co-ordinates into the computer. I run through our combat checklist; IFF is squawking, combat plug is on, the weapons are armed and programmed and the ECM, RWR and expendables are on line. We turn towards the attack heading and accelerate to combat speed.

'After 60 seconds I call up the ANGLICO FAC and tell them to turn their laser on, and they begin to "paint" the target. I turn on my ARBS/DMT, and because (from the nine-line brief) I know basically where the target is located, I select the "narrow band" scan pattern and designate the target. This tells the DMT, using the Harrier's INS, where to look for the artillery tubes. We are now ingressing at 20,000 feet, 480 knots, and I see in my HUD that the target is acquired and locked up as the scanning DMT picks up the reflected laser energy from the ANGLICO team, and I now start getting range information from the target. Three and a half miles out, I roll in for a steep delivery, pulling 4g on the way down. My wingman takes high cover; he tells me my six o'clock is clear. I'm accelerating rapidly to 600 knots, 45-degree angle, 15,000 feet. I see the target below me, I tell the FAC I'm wings level and he gives me a "Clear and hot" call. Because I have laser lock, I go for an automatic delivery.

'I depress the "pickle" button and I get a "bomb fall line" appearing in my HUD. I fly the aircraft on to the vertical line, and as my release cue appears I start a gentle pull-up to the cue. I get a tone in my headset and the bombs are away. My wingman hears the tone and knows my bombs are gone; he gives me an updated threat call as I climb away and he tells me he's to my right 4 o'clock. I call "Visual on you, you're clear" and he rolls in for his attack as I take high cover.

'He can see my bombs going off, and the FAC also calls a good hit on the primary target and tells him to "Correct west 200 metres from Lead's hit." He rogers that call and rolls wings-level. He's in the chute, and because the laser is now obscured by smoke he switches to CCIP in his HUD. Now he only gets "Cross-hairs", so he drags the lines across the target and hits the pickle button.

'From my vantage point I am looking at the flashes on the ground. Could be triple-A; could be SAMs. I hear his bomb-release tone, and from the north I see a whole bunch of zaps coming up. I call "Triple-A nine o'clock, jink right . . . Come hard right 90 degrees." He's now pumping out chaff and flares to defeat any missile threat as he power-climbs out. A good strike, no problems, both okay, so we quickly re-join an egress to Tanajib for a quick turnaround.'

'After a rolling landing on the alum-matted site, and while the aircraft are rearmed and refuelled—this time with six excellent Rockeye cluster bomb units—we grab a bite to eat, a quick intel check and back into the air. Now we are flying "alert" in a holding pattern, having told the DASC we are airborne and available. We are advised that an airborne FAC in an F-18 "Delta" has a job for us as he has made contact with a convoy of Iraqi trucks moving north. He reads us the nine-line brief and we follow him into the target zone. I pick him up visually as he rolls in for a mark. I see the flash as he launches a nine-inch Zuni rocket with a white phosphorus warhead.

'The smoke from the oil fires is pretty intense in these areas so we have to attack from a lower altitude, this time 10,000 feet. We see the Delta pull off, popping flares, and as we roll in I squeeze off a long burst of 25mm shells, spraying the area and putting high-explosive rounds across the trucks to keep the defenders' heads down. I line the jet up and switch to CCIP, select a vehicle in the cross-hairs and hit the "pickle" button. The CBUs are programmed to separate in the same manner as the bombs carried earlier. The six canisters leave the wing stations, creating a "footprint of devastation" as they hit. My wingman follows in to complete the attack. During both strikes the F-18 Delta is giving constant threat calls as we pull off . . .

'Another successful day for the Marines Harriers as we turn away into the blue desert sky and head home.'

'FASTASS CAS'

The F-16 Fighting Falcon has long been admired as a genuine multi-mission strike fighter. To enhance its undoubted reputation further, work continues to be undertaken to modify the aircraft into a dedicated close air support platform, and the task of bringing the CAS role to the F-16 has been allocated the 174th Fighter Wing's 138th Fighter Squadron, of the New York Air National Guard— 'The Boys from Syracuse'. With their aircraft now designated F/A-16 (fighter/attack) to denote its new status, the 'Boys' have a surprise or two built into their Electric Jets.

It is the heat of battle, and smoke, fires and confusion reign. CAS is required by the Army, and on the ground a hard-pressed FAC has the job of talking in a strike aircraft he probably cannot see and a pilot he can only just hear. Laser may be inappropriate because of the smoke, so it's all down to verbal communications—a tall order, and one certainly open to misinterpretation. Enter a new system being pioneered by the F/A-16—ATHS, standing for Automatic Target Handoff System. ATHS is one of a number of avionics changes made

to the F/A-16, but it is probably the most significant as it provides an electronic link between the pilot and the ground. Using ATHS, a FAC can enter data into a portable system and at the push of a button the whole scenario is presented to the pilot, showing him the target type, elevation and latitude/ longitude, these references all appearing in his HUD. In a split second ATHS has eliminated any inaccurate verbal communications. Captain Jeffrey Ecker, or 'X', a Flight Commander with the 138th, an experienced CAS flyer and a Vietnam and Gulf War veteran as well as a graduate of the USAF's Aggressor School, explains:

'The name of the game is to hit the target with the first pass and avoid getting hit. The F/A-16 is rugged, small and agile, and it allows us to move quickly in and out of the threat envelope, and using our ATHS it gives us a greater accuracy and survivability factor because we do not have to scan for a target or have to make judgements based on a ground agency's communications.

'Here at Syracuse we were given the job of evaluating the F-16 as a CAS airplane, and then "writing

Captain Jeffrey Ecker
Jeff Ecker is a 39-year-old Pennsylvanian, married and with two daughters. He has spent most of his active duty abroad flying the A-10 and all models of the F-16, at bases as far flung as Bentwaters in the United Kingdom and Suwon in Korea. He was one of the first to fly the F-16 in the 'aggressor' role at RAF Alconbury, and he joined the Syracuse Air Guard in 1990 at the end of his active flying career.

His current 'day job' is as a pilot with United Airlines, and this is a position which allows him to maintain his commitment to the ANG. 'I found it ironic that in all the years I was on active duty preparing for war nothing happened,' he remarks. 'I retire, join the 138th as a part-timer and I'm off to the Gulf!'

He adds: 'The 138th . . . continues to prove the worth of the F-16 in the CAS role. As can be seen from our Gulf experience, it is a continuing re-evaluation of the "system", so that we can be that one step ahead at all times. It must be said that, in any future conflict, if we are called to duty, the last thing the enemy will want to see, or probably will see, is "The Boys from Syracuse"!'

'The Boys from Syracuse'

Below: Flying low over the New York countryside. The scenery is reminiscent of what can be found in Europe, and so 'The Boys' have sectioned off the state map to represent areas of a possible European conflict. For example, the Czech border runs along the edge of the Adriondack Mountains! (Photo: Lockheed)

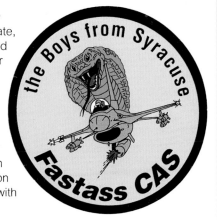

'The Boys from Syracuse' and the 138th

Flying out of Hancock Field in central New York state, the 'Boys' have, over their 45-year history, have had to contend with 'older' aircraft—like so many other ANG units. In terms of hardware, however, the year 1979 was something of a watershed, when they were equipped with the A-10 Thunderbolt, putting them, for the first time, on a par with other front-line units. In 1988 twenty-six early F-16A aircraft were assigned to the unit to begin the process of evaluating them for CAS, and eighteen of these jets were deployed to the Gulf for Operation "Desert Storm". The story continues for the 138th with their recent transition to the F/A-16C.

'FASTASS CAS'

Above: High above the clouds with the 'boss's bird': a rare shot of the aircraft toting the General Electric Gepod 30mm cannon, the same weapon as that found on the A-10. Used during 'Desert Storm', the gun now has an uncertain future with the F/A-16. (Photo: Lockheed)

the book" on its employment and tactics. It was obvious early on in the programme that the jet was well suited to the task, although originally we were only given examples of the early A model, with all its inherent problems (for an F-16), but we are now transitioning to the much more capable and user-friendly C model, which has all of the updates and avionic systems we lacked with our early birds. The addition of ATHS and the capability to carry and use the LANTRIN system has given our new F/A-16s even more impressive abilities.'

The 'Boys from Syracuse' are no strangers to CAS, having for nearly ten years flown the A-10 Warthog in the ground attack role and being regularly deployed to Europe, where they continued to

Firing 'The Gun'

'In the F/A-16A we had to visually aim the gun using a traditional "reticle" in the HUD, manually calculating the lead for target and slant ranges. Thankfully, now, with our new C models we have a CCIP displayed, and this has dramatically improved the accuracy of the weapon.' However, 'using the gun took us lower into the threat environment, and it was 'carried . . . into battle on the third day of the war only, firing it manually and "stirring it around" using lots of rudder.' (Gavin McLeod)

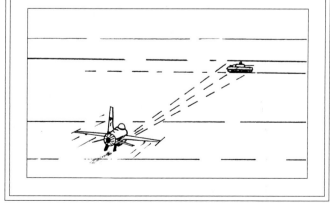

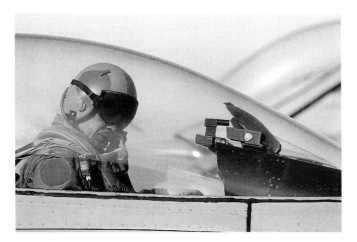

Above left: Jeff Ecker runs through the cockpit checklist for his F/A-16 at the home of 'FastAss Cas', Hancock Field. (Photo: Author)

Above right: Despite an aircraft's computer-driven systems, a good map is always advisable for any CAS mission! To provide more realistic training, the State map has been divided up to represent Europe! (Photo: Author)

Below: Making a stop-over to share the Syracuse ramp are visitors from Shaw AFB. (Photo: Author)

hone and fine-tune their skills in the event of an East/West conflict. Their success and approach did not go unnoticed at Command level, and their expertise and experience with CAS made them the ideal choice to take on the challenge of the F-16.

'When working CAS,' continues Jeff Ecker, 'one of our weapons of choice has been the 30mm Avenger gun of A-10 fame, and we can carry a compact, pod-mounted version, the GE GPU-5/A. This gives us

Left: Chocks are pulled as Jeff Ecker prepares to taxi out. (Photo: Author)

Below: A two-seat F/A-16B trainer on strength with the Syracuse ANG. (Photo: Mike Kopack)

Right: Going up! The sun glints off the canopy of an F/A-16 as it 'pulls the vertical'. With the F-16 already proven as a multi-mission aircraft, the 138th FW were given the task of adding CAS to its impressive repertoire. (Lockheed)

attack options roughly similar to those of the Hog. In the F/A-16A we had to visually aim the gun using a traditional "reticle" in the HUD, manually calculating the lead for target and slant ranges. Thankfully, now, with our new C models we have a CCIP displayed, and this has dramatically improved the accuracy of the weapon.

'We also make use of cluster bombs, standard "iron" bombs and Maverick missiles, and of course we continue to carry the ever-comforting AIM-9s on the wing tips. The training and tactics we developed in our A models was put to the acid test in 1991 when our specialized brand of CAS was deployed to the Gulf during "Desert Storm". We were not the

Left: Jeff Ecker taxies out an as yet unmarked F/A-16. (Photo: Author)

Below: Being so close to the 'top edge' of the United States, winter can be pretty severe at Syracuse. The scene is a frosty morning at Hancock Field as the morning light catches the tail and Sidewinder of one of 'The Boys from Syracuse'. (Photo: Mike Waters)

only F-16 units tasked with ground attack or close air support, but we felt we had an edge due to the fact that we regularly train with the Army and their FACs, we were used to the environment and we knew what they wanted and how to respond to their needs.

'Sadly, because of all the additional software needed to operate our F/A-16s in the desert, the computer system was soon saturated and something had to give, so reluctantly we went into battle without our trusty ATHS. Tactics and weapon loadings were then modified to suit our missions, but we soon found that a satisfactory mix was to use a four-jet combination for attack sorties. Each jet carried two AIM-9s, two 370-gallon tanks and an ALQ-199 jammer; two were armed with Mk 82 slick bombs and two with either Mavericks or CBUs, depending on the target.

'We carried the gun-pod into battle on the third day of the war only, firing it manually and "stirring it around" using lots of rudder. It was ironic that on this day we had our only "casualty" of the conflict, when Major Dennis Miller's aircraft had a SAM explode a few inches off his right wing tip. Although the jet was peppered with holes and leaking fuel,

Major Miller managed, with the aid of his wingman, to limp the aircraft back to a friendly base.

'Using the gun took us lower into the threat environment, and because it was perceived that there was now no real need to go that low, we didn't carry the 30mm for the rest of the war. Not before one of our four ships had the dubious honour of chasing some Iraqi jeeps around an airfield, taking some of the more bizarre kills of the war. We also discovered that one of the best weapons available to us was the CBU-87. However, our computer was not programmed to deliver it, so we had to "lie" to the system and tell it we had some CBU-52s on board and manually compensate for the offsets. Good though the weapon was, we could not get the accuracy we wanted and decided to stop carrying it. We did find, however, that a Mk 84 bomb with a radar proximity fuse was nearly equal to a cluster bomb, creating significant damage from its fragments.

'Our chief role in "Desert Storm" was to undertake second-echelon strikes against the Republican Guard in Kuwait, and using our standard "package" we would be employed against artillery or bunkers. We flew the aircraft hard, almost up to their 40,000lb limits, using a take-off roll in excess of 8,000 feet. We also developed mission-planning cells at our Al Kharj base, and we would spend hours poring over our allotted tasks. Once airborne with the co-ordinates to take us in to the target area, we would begin to work the ground FACs, or even sometimes visually acquire our prey with no external help. We would roll in from 20,000 feet, looking for a weapons release at about 10,000 that kept us above any triple-A and SAM threats. We developed an attack pattern that saw one aircraft flying "high cover" and one aircraft flying "chase" while two attacked the target. Once the ordnance had been delivered, they would pull off and reverse roles.

'The Mavericks we carried had an excellent kill rate, but they did generate a much higher cockpit workload during an attack, as we used more "heads-

Above: The noise at Hancock Field can get deafening during intense operations with all 'The Boys" jets wound up. Here a crew chief checks over his charge, the intercom giving him direct contact with the pilot above the din. (Photo: Author)

Below: In full flying kit, Jeff Ecker checks out the practice bombs on the stores pylon of his F/A-16. (Photo: Author)

in" time to set up the missile. We fired 73 of the IR version and in those moments our cover/chase tactics were invaluable.'

By the time these words reach print the 138th will be at full strength with their "new" F/A-16Cs, and in the light of their Gulf experiences new tactics and aircraft development continue apace. More emphasis will now be placed on the delivery of precision guided weapons from higher altitudes, and evaluation continues as to what future, if any, the 30mm gun-pod will have in operations.

SCREAMIN' EAGLES

At precisely 2.38 a.m. on 17 January 1991, laser-guided Hellfire missiles launched from eight Army AH-64 Apache helicopters began ripping apart two early warning/intercept sites in far western Iraq. These simultaneous attacks were mounted by elements of the 101st Airborne's 101st Aviation Division, 1st Battalion, 101st Aviation Regiment. Working in conjunction with US Air Force Pave Low 'pathfinders', the 'Screamin' Eagles' struck the first blows of 'Desert Storm'. Flying in complete darkness and using their passive FLIR sensors, the Apaches stalked their prey. At the appointed moment the 'fire commands' were sounded. Tuning in on invisible laser beams squirted from the helicopters, the Hellfire missiles angled

Right, upper: During 'Desert Storm' the Apache proved to be an excellent warrior, accounting for the first strike of the conflict and then maintaining an 80 per cent readiness rate during its operations. (Photo: McDonnell Douglas)

Right, lower: Called in by the Kiowa scouts, an Apache makes a dash across a clearing. (Photo: Mike Verier)

Far right: Nose-mounted electronic wizardry, Hellfire missiles, rockets and 1,200 rounds of high explosive shell— to be treated with the utmost respect! (Photo: McDonnell Douglas)

down and exploded on their targets, creating white 'bursts' in the tiny 'green screens' of the TV tabs inside the helos. Salvos of 2.75in rockets were launched, scattering thousands of razor sharp flechettes as they hit home. Buildings crumbled beneath the pounding of missiles, aided by the

101st Airborne Division

The 101st Airborne Division can trace its lineage back to the 101st Division, which was formed on 23 July 1918. Since that time the famous 'Screamin' Eagles' have proved their steel from the D-Day beaches through Vietnam to the Gulf. The 101st shoulder patch shows an American bald eagle on a black shield, beneath an 'Airborne' tab. The emblem was adopted in 1923 by the 101st Infantry Division when it was based in the state of Wisconsin. The eagle's head represents 'Old Abe', the mascot of the 8th Wisconsin Infantry Regiment which was carried into battle during the American Civil War.

AH-64 Apache

impacting rounds from the Apaches' 30mm chain guns. Within 30 seconds the sites were disabled; within four minutes every piece of equipment, barracks and vehicles had been destroyed. Moments later came the eerie sound of hundreds of fighters, bombers and cruise missiles funnelling down the newly created radar-black 'corridor', heading, undetected, to their targets. 'Out of the darkness we had hit the Iraqis with a force they could not see and with technology they did not understand.'

The McDonnell Douglas Apache had come of age. It has always been considered one of the most

Above: The 2.25in rockets can be fired in various salvo patterns and can be linked to the laser rangefinder for precise aiming. The engine exhaust plume suppressors and the AN/ALQ-144 'disco lights' IR jammer add to the survivability of the aircraft against heat-seeking missiles. (Photo: McDonnell Douglas)

potent weapons systems in the world, and one of the most flexible assets on the battlefield. CW2 Duane Crawford, from Alpha Company of the 101st Airborne Division, 2-101st Aviation Regiment, continues:

'Here at the 2-101st our primary task is to kill tanks, and that's what the Apache does better than anything else. We are also the "manoeuvre" element on the battlefield, providing security and deep-strike capabilities for the 101st Air Assault Division, and because we have proven now the abilities of the Apache, we are also taking over a lot of the traditional "cavalry" roles from the Cobra gunships.'

Built by McDonnell Douglas, the Apache is specifically a twin-engine, four-blade multi-mission attack helicopter, and, carrying a 'battle rostered' crew of two (pilot-in-command, or PIC, and co-pilot/gunner, or CPG), it was developed to undertake

battlefield sorties by day or night and in adverse weather. It carries an enviable array of weapon sensors which feature the specialized TADS target acquisition system, containing a laser, direct-view optics and a FLIR. This is combined with the AAQ-11 Pilot's Night Vision System, or PNVS, and together these sensors endow the Apache with a commanding view of the night and allow a target to be either manually or automatically tracked once it has been acquired by the CPG. The sensors are mounted in the nose of the aircraft, giving it a distinctive 'warty' appearance.

Another feature of the Apache is the pilot's Integrated Helmet and Display System, IHADS, which consists of a monocular tube, the HDU (Helmet Display Unit), and is clipped to the PIC's helmet, presenting him with a 'patch' of thermal imaging which is projected on to a small glass screen in front of his right eye. Electrical contacts fitted to his helmet also allow him to slew the nose-mounted sensors and chain gun to his line of sight.

The aircraft carries a number of self-defence aids such as chaff and flare launchers, radar warning receiver and infra-red jammer, but it is its offensive abilities that make it such a deadly opponent. Up to sixteen lethal Hellfire missiles can be toted, along with pods containing up to seventy-six 70mm rockets, while the 1,200-round, nose-mounted 30mm

Right: AH-64A Apache general configuration.

Below left: The flat plate windshield is very evident in this view. (Photo: Mike Kopack)

Below right: The PIC (pilot-in-command: rear seat) and the CPG (co-pilot/gunner: front seat) begin their numerous checks before winding up the engines. The pilot's-helmet mounted IHADS monocle is visible on his 'bone-dome'. (Photo: Mike Verier)

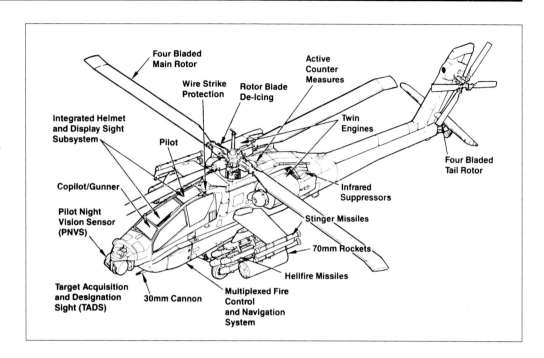

Four Bladed Main Rotor

Wire Strike Protection

Rotor Blade De-Icing

Active Counter Measures

Integrated Helmet and Display Sight Subsystem

Pilot

Twin Engines

Copilot/Gunner

Four Bladed Tail Rotor

Pilot Night Vision Sensor (PNVS)

Infrared Suppressors

Stinger Missiles

70mm Rockets

Hellfire Missiles

Target Acquisition and Designation Sight (TADS)

30mm Cannon

Multiplexed Fire Control and Navigation System

cannon can be fired by either crewman. Power is provided by two General Electric T700-GE-701C turboshafts, with unique infra-red suppressors fitted to their exhausts, and these powerplants each deliver 1,800shp. Protection for the crew is enhanced by the use of armour plating around their positions.

'At the 101st, being involved in air assault, we have, in addition to the anti-tank role, the anti-armour/anti-artillery role, which requires us to go beyond the FLOT [forward line of troops] to attack maybe an armoured column or perhaps artillery "tubes" that could be impeding our infantry,' continues Crawford. 'We are also heavily involved with air assault security, when we ensure that all of the LZs [landing zones] are "clear and cold" before assault divisions put their infantry into the area.

'Because we have to consider not only our own objectives but the objectives of the infantry, mission briefs are very comprehensive. We look at our

formation, laser codes, weapons configuration, MOP posture (mission-oriented protection—in case of nuclear/biological attack), pick-up levels in case one of us goes down, time lines, relative positions of friendly troops and what they are expecting of us in the BP.

'When we move out to the helo we have with us our LC vest containing our survival gear, radios, first aid, water, knives, mirrors, fish-hooks etc.; we also have our NBC kit, and I like to take a rucksack with a sleeping bag just in case we go down and have to wait a while for a pick-up. We also have body armour available to us as necessary. Pre-flight is broken into two areas, the PIC taking the tail to front on the right, the CPG the front to tail from the left.

'Once happy, the PIC climbs into the back seat, the CPG into the front, and we buckle up our five-point harnesses. Both make sure the respective cockpit switches are "safe" and all circuit-breakers

and power levers are off. The PIC throws the battery switch and checks his caution/warning panel and then ensures the fire detectors all work, checking also his comms to the CPG.

'PIC then cranks up the APU (auxiliary power unit) and will get an "On" light, after which the

Left: The pilot's 'office'. (Photo: McDonnell Douglas)

Right: Having been checked over by the ground crew, the Apache team secure themselves into their aircraft and begin the procedures that wind up their high-tech systems. (Photo: Mike Verier)

Far right: Duane Crawford demonstrates the IHADS that clips on to his flying helmet. (Photo: 101 Airborne)

Left: A raiding pair of AH-64As performing a 'pop-up and fire' manoeuvre with 2.75in rockets. (Photo: Mike Verier)

the Air Data Sensor System, his symbol generator, his TADS and the IHADS. When all this is complete, the PIC switches up the PNVS. The CPG then enters in his eight-digit present-position grid off the GPS into the FCC and announces to the pilot "Present-position is in." He then turns on the HARS (Heading and Attitude Reference System) which takes around 6–9 minutes to align.

'The CPG is now busy putting all of the waypoints into the doppler, punching in the laser codes, checking that all the correct indications are coming up in the weapons systems and entering any positional data into his "deck". Once the HARS is fixed, the PIC calls "Coming hot on number one" and proceeds to crank up the first of the engines. He throws the start switch, looks for the fuel boost pump light and pass-air cut off, and monitors the NG speed. Once that comes up to 22 per cent, the power lever goes to "Idle" and he watches the turbine gas temperatures. He then calls "Comes hot on number two", making sure that the TGS does not exceed 852. Once hot on, both the power levers are set to "Fly" at 100 per cent. The pre-take off "hit checks" are then run, and the bird is ready to go.

generators come on line. Once these are working he goes about switching on all the other systems. He checks the DASE (Digital Automatic Stabilization Equipment) gear, radar detector, IR jammer, avionics, radios and rad-alt and uncages the attitude indicator; the CPG meanwhile is turning on

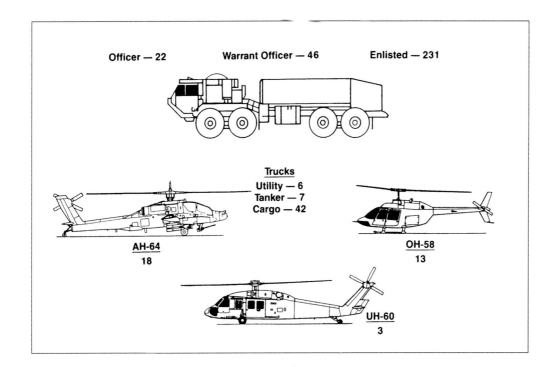

Left: Composition of an Apache battalion.

Right, upper: Feeding the 30mm chain gun is a demanding task. Here the ground crew have the shells laid out prior to 'up-loading' them into the aircraft. (Photo: Mike Verier)

Right, lower: A close view of the Rockwell AGM-114A Hellfire missile, which can be used to engage several targets in quick succession with devastating results. (Photo: Curtiss Knowles)

'Because the Apache has basically two separate cockpits, each occupant has his own set of rules to work by, except when ready to take off and the CGG and PIC confirm the HARS is operating, the DASE is engaged and the weapons are on line. The PIC calls in a systems check and the CPG reads off fuel, caution/warning panel etc. and confirms the engine rotor instruments are all in the green. At the call "Power check" the PIC turns the Apache in the direction of take-off and comes to a 5-foot hover, noting the engine torque and confirming that with the CPG.

'In Alpha Company our call-signs are "Highlander" for tactical use, but in order to remain as much "comm-out" as possible we use pre-determined code-words to indicate to the formation our procedures. For example, on take-off the lead might call "Turbo". Ten seconds later he will depart, with the formation falling in behind him at the appropriate spacing. The trail aircraft will then call "Booster" once he is airborne, which informs everyone that the birds are all flying. Speed out is generally 100kts if we are operating with the '58s or up to 120kts if we are Apache only.

'Towards the BP we adopt a "staggered right" formation, and as we hit the low-level ingress phase, when we use valleys and hills to mask our target approach, we configure to "free cruise". As we near the BP, around 3km out Lead will call "Slowing". The scouts go on ahead to clear our path, and once established they call us in and assume responsibility for our close-in security.

'One of the biggest assets in the Apache is its night fighting abilities, and this centres around the PNVS (Pilot's Night Vision System), which is basically a FLIR, presenting a green picture to him through the monocular Helmet Display Sight, and this is connected to the IHADS. In the front the CPG has a similar view through his TADS, seeing what the pilot sees, but he has the advantage of using his ORT (optical ray tube), slaving it to fixed-forward, zooming in or out using four fields of vision, wide, medium, narrow or long, giving him up to 126 power optics.

'If one of our scouts calls in "Taking fire", we can quickly suppress this by using the 30mm gun slaved to the IHADS, laying a carpet of fire on the position. Once we are established at the BP we go about the

business of picking out our targets using the TADS, and if tanks are present we prepare to engage them with our Hellfire missiles.

'The Hellfire is really an easy system. Using the TADS, the CPG zooms in to make the target look as big as possible, he squirts it with the laser to the first detent, and this gives the range, and he then tells the pilot he has a tank "Within range" and is firing "One missile off the left-hand side". He squirts the laser to the second detent, which designates the target, and launch constraints appear in the TADS. This is basically a "box" covering the target. If this is "dashed", the missile is out of constraints; if it is "solid", we are ready to roll. He calls "Solid box" and squeezes the trigger, and calls a good launch. The Hellfire locks on to the reflected laser energy and the target is history.

'Using the chain gun is also a simple procedure, and there is no real co-ordination needed to fire: it follows your head, or can be used with the TADS. The CPG initiates the gun using his WAS (Weapon Activation System) and he gets a gun message in the bottom right of his picture with a notation of the available rounds.

'Our time at a target area is a large variable. If it's a direct attack on a known target, fifteen minutes should be enough to see us empty of rounds, or "Winchester" (our call for "rounds out"). In an air assault scenario we may be on task for 40–45 minutes while our Blackhawks and heavy-lifters bring troops and material into the LZ. If we need longer on station we use a phased attack—that means one company on task, one en route and another at a FARP getting gassed and armed up.

'Egress routes are always planned to give us an exit in a different direction to our entry, and these can be timed in conjunction with our artillery, so they can give us a barrage of covering fire.

'I love flying the Apache. It is a superb platform, and I don't know of another system as capable of killing tanks as efficiently as we can. My opinion is that all Army pilots are 'élite' simply by the nature of the job they do.'

CAS, FAC AND NIGHT ATTACK

'**W**e are the Corps' jack-of-all-trades as we possess the only aircraft in the current inventory that is able to provide five of the six functions demanded of Marine aviation. There are few aircraft that are as capable and as flexible as our "birds". We can fly CAP (combat air patrol) as fighters, carry HARM missiles as SEAD (suppression of enemy air defences) electronic warfare platforms, carry out reconnaissance, perform night attack missions using our comprehensive sensors and goggles, and conduct FAC-A (forward air controller-airborne) duties. Possibly, however, it is the FAC work that has gained us the greatest fame and recognition over the deserts of Iraq and in the skies above Bosnia. We have a true multi-mission capability. Literally, we can, at the flick of a switch, turn

Below: Following a 'Hornet High' manoeuvre, a 'Bengals Delta' tips over for a simulated CAS run during a 'Deny Flight' mission over Bosnia. A check on the stores reveals, left to right, AIM-9, 5in rocket pod, fuel tank, targeting FLIR, 500lb Mk 82 bomb, TINS pod, fuel tank, Mk 82 bomb and AIM-9. (Photo: J. Papay)

VMFA(AW)-224
First established as Marine All Weather Fighter Attack Squadron 224 on 1 May 1942, the unit received two Presidential Citations for action in the Guadalcanal and Marshall Islands campaigns. Since then the 'Bengals' have continued to serve with distinction, flying aircraft such as the Banshee, Panther, Skyhawk and, more recently, Intruder. During 1992 VMA(AW)-224 celebrated its fiftieth anniversary and also traded the last of its A-6s to the Navy during that March, taking on charge the 'missionized' F/A-18D, moving to Beaufort in South Carolina and being re-designated VMFA(AW)-224.

F/A-18D Hornet

Above: One of the 'Bengals' heads back to Aviano AFB at the end of an exhausting 4½-hour CAP mission over Bosnia. (Photo: J. Papay)

Left: 'Wizzo' Captain Mark 'Jocko' Johnson 'flies' a Walleye TV-guided bomb using his hand controllers and MFDs following its release by Captain Derek 'Chisel' Richardson. (Photo: Richardson)

from fighter to bomber, from spotter to aggressor, and our systems can turn night into day'—a keen appraisal of the fighting abilities of the US Marine Corps' latest acquisition, the 'missionized' two-seat F/A-18 'Delta' by Captain Gregg 'Kramer' Heines and Captain Gary 'Gumby' Graham of VMFA(AW)-224, the 'Fighting Bengals' from MCAS Beaufort in South Carolina.

'The two-seat concept of the F/A-18D has put an extra set of eyes in the aircraft, which is vital in the FAC-A role, and during hazardous night attack profiles, when the pilot is heavily involved in keeping above the dirt! We have instances in the Gulf

War where the back-seater made the difference between being hit and avoiding a missile,' explains Gary Graham. 'Up front, the pilot has control of the jet, but it's in the back seat, where the WSO, or Wizzo, operates the sophisticated sensors and nav equipment, that the impressive capabilities of this aircraft can be appreciated.

'We call our back-seaters WSOs, but, unlike the Air Force designation, in the Marines it stands for weapons and sensor operator, not weapons system officer. The WSO's cockpit operates independently of the pilot's, allowing him to optimize his information to suit the task ahead. Two MFDs (multi-function displays, also referred to as DDT, for digital display terminals) occupy the left and right portions of his front panel, with a computer-generated, full colour moving-map display high on the centre section. The WSO accesses the computer and controls the sensors by two joysticks situated at his left and right hands and soft-key function buttons around and above his MFDs.

'Sensors in the Delta include a "strap-on" Loral AN/AAS-38 targeting FLIR pod, containing a laser designator and ranger, and a Hughes AN/AAR-50 thermal imaging navigation system (TINS). This is what we call our NAVFLIR, and it can project its image into the pilot's Marconi HUD. Both of these items are mounted on the intake Sparrow stations. The FLIR generates an excellent TV picture, allowing us to operate on the blackest of nights and giving a 'warm and fuzzy feeling', as we call it, enabling us to fly at 500 feet or below at high jet speeds.

'The F/A-18D—our aircraft are from the latest Block 17—has the updated APG-73 radar with superb air-to-air and air-to-ground properties and is powered by two General Electric F404-GE-402 enhanced-performance engines (EPEs), each delivering 18,000lb of thrust, making us an agile and potent platform that can carry any mix of weaponry in the files.

'We can fly single- or multi-ship missions, and during "Deny Flight" over Bosnia we operated our FAC-A and close air support mission with two aircraft, one acting as the FAC, the other as CAS support. We were flattered that the commanders on the spot specifically asked for the Delta Hornets to be deployed to the area because of our unique knowledge and familiarity with the CAS mission, combined with our night sensors and night operating abilities. We owned the hours between 6.00 p.m. and 4.00 a.m.—the night belonged to the Deltas as we patrolled the skies. Not even the F-15E Strike Eagles were able to undertake the type of mission we did. The F-15E is an excellent aircraft, but it's not as flexible as the F/A-18D.

Right, upper: The rear cockpit of the F/A-18D. Notice the MFDs and the hand controllers. The UFC is 'like a push button telephone'. (Photo: Heines)

Right, lower: A view of the Cat's Eyes NVGs worn by the crews of the F/A-18Ds. (Photo: Heines)

Far right, upper: Captain Gary 'Gumby' Graham briefs an air-to-air mission. (Photo: Author)

Far right, lower: 'Pre-flighting' their aircraft are Lieutenant-Colonel Dan 'Wombat' Kernen, and Captain Jerry 'Fish' Christensen. Both airmen are paying attention to the disposition of their Walleye glide bomb. (Photo: Heines)

'Briefings are generally one and a half hours prior to take-off, and we look at every aspect of the mission, especially the weather, our fuel and who we will be dealing with. Once completed, we walk to the jets, having first picked up our kit, which includes G-suit, torso harness and SV2, which is unique to the Navy and Marines as it is a survival vest with flotation gear that deploys on contact with salt water. Having signed for the jets, we move to the pan for the pre-flights. The pilot is the first on board, and, once settled, he kicks in the APU and, after checking out his systems, winds up the engines. Once we get 60 per cent rpm the gear begins to come on line very quickly and we are soon ready to roll.

'One of the real beauties of the F/A-18D for me as a pilot is that while I am running my checks the Wizzo is able to input his information independently, so speeding up the whole process. With the start sequence away, I sweep through my checks. Each pilot has his own method. I like to start on my left panel with the two mission computers, check the OBOGS (on-board oxygen generating system) and fuel control panel. We usually fly with a centreline tank, but during "Deny Flight" we also carried two wing tanks, giving us an additional

16,800lb of gas, allowing for around three and a half hours' unrefuelled flight time. Also on the left are the throttles, which are HOTAS [hands-on-throttle-and-stick], and with that I can use the radar (sweep/range) designate targets, control communications and use my expendables (chaff/flares). Further along I check the electrical controls and master arm and check the "Master-Mode" switch which drives the mission computer in air-to-air or air-to-ground, dependent on the scenario.

'Looking forward, I have three nine-inch MFDs, and just above the centre display is our UFC, used to input data to the computer. The displays have twenty buttons around their edges and the centre display is our MPCD, which contains the colour moving map and navigational data, INS cue and time lines. The other MFDs display their information in a monochrome green. I move across to the right console and the generator switches, battery switch, ECS (environmental control system), cabin pressure switch and temperature control. I check and set up the radios and check the panel that controls the external sensors we have fitted and lastly, on the right, the controls for the radar, which is our primary sensor.'

'In the back seat,' continues Gregg Heines, 'I first turn up my RWR and Sidewinder tones, and as soon as the battery is on line I do a comms check with the pilot. With the engines running, I check through the MFDs and MPCD, accessing the menus to input the lat/long and elevation of our present position, which is what we call "waypoint zero". I inform the pilot of this and he winds up the INS. I check the caution and warning panel and begin to enter the mission parameters, and I can include as many as 70 waypoints if necessary. The system can draw us a course line that we call the "yellow brick road", which joins up all of the waypoints—which is pretty useful. I set up the "soft and hard bugs" in the rad-alt and set the time in the HUD. I dial in the IFF squawk and TACAN and check the BIT page on the MFD's menu. I then square up the ALE-39 chaff and flare dispensers, test the oxygen and check the

Above: Sister-unit to the 'Bengals' is the 'Vikings' of VMFA(AW)-225, based at El Toro, and one of its number here demonstrates the target-marking technique using a 5in rocket. Note the false canopy painted on the underside of the aircraft. (Photo: McDonnell Douglas)

Right: 'Routinely we take on extra gas from one of our KC-130 Hercules tankers', or from a USAF KC-135 (as shown here) or KC-10. (Photo: Heines)

fuel and standby gyro, finally confirming the datum point on the moving map.'

'With our checks complete and engines running,' continues Gary Graham, 'our pins are stowed, our NVGs are safe and we are ready to go. The Plane Captain gives us the thumbs-up, the Wizzo calls up the tower and the ATIS and with clearance we taxy to the end of the runway.

'Our all-up weight is in the order of 39,000lb—that's with the sensors, fuel and weapons load—

Captain Gregg 'Kramer' Heines

Gregg Heines (above left) joined the Marines from school at the age of eighteen, serving with the reserves for eight years before gaining his commission in 1989. After training as a Naval Flight Officer, he was selected as a WSO on the F/A-18D, and following a course with the Marines training unit VMFAT-101 he joined the 'Bengals' in 1993.

Captain Gary 'Gumby' Graham

Gary Graham (above right) is a 33-year-old pilot with over twelve years' experience flying with the Marines. He has flown the A-6 Intruder on two tours with VMA(AW)-533, which included an embarkation on the USS *John F. Kennedy*, before he converted to the F/A-18D operating with VMFA(AW)-121, the first Marines 'Delta' unit.

and once again the Plane Captain gives us a final look over before we "go flying". As we reach the runway threshold we take note of the arrester gear that is situated at both ends of the runway and can be found at all Navy and Marine stations. This is very useful if we have an emergency and can't stop the jet, and catching the cable with our tail hook can save us a trip into the weeds or "goin' fourwheelin'", as we call it.

'We halt for final checks, with each aircrew member looking out and over the others' aircraft, taking a final visual check. We then position for a "ten-second go". Lead signals "Go", and power is applied and the two-plane section rolls. We accelerate smoothly to 150 knots for rotate, and once airborne, literally a few feet off the ground, Lead nods for gear and flaps up and the jets climb out steadily to 25,000 feet at 300 knots. We nearly always fly a defensive "combat spread" formation, abeam each other, positioned for the best mutual support.

'Routinely we take on extra gas from one of our KC-130 Hercules tankers, and we are also able to utilize the Air Force's KC-10 and KC-135s, and during 'Deny Flight' we also hooked up with the RAF and their TriStar tankers. The KC-130s trail two "baskets" for us to use our built-in probes on, and they are usually hangin' around at 17,000 feet doing 200 to 220 knots, which is very slow. However, our F/A-18s have automatic flight controls, which allow us to easily maintain that sort of rate. Gas-up at the "self-serve" (so called because we do the work, unlike the Air Force who have a "full serve", with someone else doing the work for them) takes five minutes and we break contact and continue to the target area.'

Top left: A HARM-equipped F/A-18D checks out, ready to roll. (Photo: J. Papay)

Top right: Maintenance crews hook up 'Bengal 505' in order to move it from the hangar. Note the engine FOD covers. (Photo: Author)

Above: In the front seat, Major 'Spanky' Benson and his WSO Captain 'Kramer' Heines start up their jet for an air-to-air mission. (Photo: Author)

'If we plan to hit a high-threat environment,' explains Gregg Heines, 'we like to go in at 500 feet or lower to avoid the radar, and one technique we use is the "pop-up attack". Basically we acquire the target with the APG-73, and then hand this off to the FLIR. About three miles from the target we pop up at twenty degrees to 2,000 feet, coming back down on to the target and delivering the ordnance in the dive. If we have difficulty in acquiring the target at that height we perform a "Hornet High", popping up at forty-five degrees to 8–10,000 feet,

F/A-18D Hornet

banking over, rolling in and delivering our load either visually if possible or by using the FLIR.

'At night we always fly with our GEC Avionics Cat's Eyes night vision goggles. These babies are $28,000 each and we treat them with the utmost respect. They give us a thirty-degree field of view, and have combiner lenses that allow us to look under them at our instruments, radar and FLIR or look up into the green night that they produce. They are so effective that we can operate our daylight tactics at night.

'Over Bosnia our goggles and FLIR were very effective sensors, as we were easily able to pick out the laser spots that the UN ground FACs were putting out and could quickly ascertain any areas of interest they wanted us to look at.

'During FAC-A missions, especially in the Gulf, the Delta was amazing. We would take off in pairs from Bahrain, one FAC and one cover, hit the tanker, check in with our assigned strike aircraft (Harriers, Hornets etc.) and proceed inbound to a "kill box", and from a high-altitude recce position pick out our designated targets, plus any other "opportunities" that came up, We exited the "kill box", picked up the strike package, led them in and then controlled them on target, in some cases firing

Below: The 'Fighting Bengals'. Back row: Captain Adam 'Cliffee' Tharp, Major Marty 'Rollo' Rollinger, Major Fred 'LC' Greenwood, Lt-Col Dan 'Wombat' Kernen, Major Mike 'Bake' McBride, Captain Derek 'Chisel' Richardson; front row: Captain Gregg 'Kramer' Heines, Captain Curt 'Buck' Rogers, Major 'Ping' Scanlon, Captain Chris 'Moe' Mahoney and Captain Harry 'Tone' Constant. (Photo: VMFA(AW)-224)

marker rockets to aid them, finishing the strike with a BDA assessment.'

'Survivability is excellent,' adds Major 'Ping' Scanlon. 'I was in an F/A-18D that was hit by an Iraqi SAM right up the tail pipe. We were pulling off a target after a strafe run when we saw the missile late—no time for flares or manoeuvres—and we promptly sucked it up the tube! We initiated an immediate climb and turned for the border, thinking we may have to eject, but the engine held together and continued to function; the afterburner petals were pretty shot but we managed the 250-mile home run!'

'Our return to base usually means a standard recovery,' continues Gary Graham, 'dependent of course on the conditions. Lead will decide on either a visual or ILS, and if all looks fair we will go for visual. Coming into the overhead in tight formation, we exercise a "break" at 1,500 feet. This is initiated at 300 to 400 knots by a crisp rolling manoeuvre, followed closely by a 6g pull to bleed off the airspeed, rolling out wings-level and descending to 1,000 feet, decelerating to 200 knots and lowering the gear and flaps. Our landing speed is around 135 to 140 knots and we report to the tower that we are "abeam with the gear down", requesting a full-stop landing.

'We gain our clearance and line up with the runway, looking for the Fresnel lens located at the touch-down point—another item found at every Marine station—so that we can practise a visual glide-slope approach, as if landing on a carrier. Right down the slope we come in to land, which in Marine and Navy terms is nothing less than a controlled crash, with a sustained rate of descent of 500 to 700 feet per minute at a constant airspeed.

'Our primary mission is to support the Marine on the ground,' concludes Gregg Heines. 'The Bengals' "Delta-Eighteens" stand ready, we have the technology and the proven abilities to own and use the night skies to our advantage, and we have an unsurpassed aircraft with which to carry out our tasks.'

105

'THE EYES OF THE TIGERS'

Having looked in detail at the standard AV-8B Harrier and its abilities, specifically in a Gulf War CAS role, and in order to bring a discussion of the Harrier's abilities up to date, we turn to the latest variant which is now entering squadron service with the Marines—the Harrier II Plus. Captain Mike 'Shooter' Richardson, of Marine Attack Squadron 542 at Cherry Point, takes up the story, and extols the virtues of the latest VSTOL jet.

'The Harrier II Plus is a major capability upgrade from the original "day attack" AV-8B and gives us a significantly greater scope of operations than even the excellent Night Attack Harrier does. The addition of several new and key systems has given our jets a much wider envelope of missions and conditions. We now have what we always wanted from the Harrier—the true capability to operate by day or night and in all weather conditions. The "Tigers" truly have their eyes.

'The most important changes are the addition of a radar, a FLIR, a colour moving map, an uprated

Captain Michael Richardson

Mike 'Shooter' Richardson is a 33-year-old Marine pilot who hails from Hamilton, Ohio, and was commissioned as a Second Lieutenant in the Marine Corps in May 1987. He attended the Basic Schooling at Quantico, Virginia, later that same year, and on completion moved to primary jet training on the T-34 in 1988. Intermediate jet training on the T-2 and advanced jet training on A-4 took place at Meridian in Mississippi from March 1989 to March 1990, following which he attended conversion training to the AV-8B in November 1990. He is currently assigned to VMA-542, where he serves as the Harrier II Plus Standardization and Instruction Officer at Cherry Point. (Photo: Author)

Harrier II Plus

Below left: A brace of 'Tigers' show off the Harrier tactical paint scheme (HTPS), the benefits of which are obvious. (Photo: McDonnell Douglas)

Right: A Harrier II Plus awaits its next sortie on the 'Tigers" ramp at Cherry Point. (Photo: Author)

Below right: An excellent vantage point to view the re-styled nose section and the yellow outlined chaff and flare dispensers on this pair of 'Plusses' from VMA-223 'Bulldogs'. (Photo: McDonnell Douglas)

engine, a card file system and a DSU (Data Storage Unit). The radar is the Hughes APG-65, already in service with the F/A-18 Hornet, and this gives us an air-to-air and air-to-ground mode, it's jam-resist-ant and it allows all-weather tracking abilities. It enables us to acquire, track and designate targets under a wide spectrum of conditions and facilitates detecting and tracking threats, weather-avoidance

Above: Something out of *Star Trek*? Not quite—in reality a close up of the night vision goggles worn by the Marine Harrier pilots and a good time to compare them with those worn by their RAF counterparts in the GR.7 section. (Photo: Author)

Above right: A quick check of the personal equipment before climbing aboard the jet. (Photo: Author)

Above far right: A camouflaged 'bone-dome' adorns this 'Tigers' pilot as he powers up his systems. (Photo: Author)

Right: Shooter' Richardson taxies his jet out to the 'Tigers" ramp, giving a good perspective of the new nose section and in particular the angular 'box' of the FLIR housing. (Photo: Author)

Far right: 'Shooter' Richardson taxies away. Note the chaff and flare launchers on the upper part of the rear fuselage. (Photo: Author)

and position-updating to name but a few of its benefits. It's also a tremendous SA (situational awareness) builder.

'The addition of a colour moving map, which is tied to the INS, has given us a "paperless cockpit" as the aircraft's position is on constant display, superimposed on the map, which advances as the aircraft moves. There are several scales available to us, from 1:1,000,000 down to 1:50,000, and any pertinent data for the mission can be placed on the map, and items such as fuel, timings, threat data, reminders and navigation cues can be marked at any position. The FLIR is mounted on top of the radome in a "box" fairing [a more angular assembly than on the RAF's GR.7], and its picture can be displayed on one of the multi-function colour displays or projected on to the HUD. This provides, in conjunction with our NVGs, the critical "window" we need to successfully operate the aircraft in the night attack profile, and we also now have NVG-compatible cockpit lighting.

'The engine is the uprated Rolls-Royce Pegasus F402-RR-408, which gives us greater thrust and, with the 100 per cent LERX [leading-edge root extensions], provides greater manoeuvring power and increased load capacity, tied in with improved HOTAS for the flight controls. Expendables (chaff and flares) capacity has been more than doubled, with the addition of two double dispensers on the upper part of the rear fuselage. The DSU has taken away the need to input flight information whilst sitting in the jet, and a card file has been integrated into the computer system to allow the pilot to "write", via a computerized planning aid, all of his mission data on to "files", which can be accessed during flight on either of the MFCDs, again eliminating the need for "paper" in the cockpit.

Above: Final clearance is given and 'Shooter' winds up the Harrier for a short take-off. (Photo: Author)

Below: The II Plus shows off its underfuselage cannon. One pod contains the ammunition, the other the gun itself, connected by a 'bridge'. (Photo: McDonnell Douglas)

Right: A Harrier II Plus from VMA-231 'Ace Of Spades', also located at Cherry Point, releases weapons in a shallow dive. (Photo: McDonnell Douglas)

Below right: Standing on its engine thrust, and using the manoeuvring 'puffers' on its four extremities, the Harrier is brought in for a vertical landing. (Photo: McDonnell Douglas)

'As with any mission, the first stage is planning, and the basis for the Harrier II Plus is that we spend time at our MOMS. That's our Maintenance Operator and Mapping Station, not one of our parents! This is basically a large-memory computer set up to calculate our timings, fuel, threat sector and navigational planning. We spend between one and three hours at our MOMS, inputting all of our mission data, using the information the computer contains. The computer then provides ingress and egress routes, fuel required, threat corridors, weaponeering, moon and sun angles, communications, IFF and flight-card load-outs. Once complete, the information is stored on a 3.5-inch floppy disk and transferred to the DSU which the pilot takes with him to his aircraft. He plugs it in and downloads all of the flight data to the jet's computer in a matter of seconds.

'Once briefed, we pick up our kit and NVGs, get them calibrated, move to the jet and get airborne. The aircraft is designed to provide mission/flight checks at all times, and it is the pilot's responsibility to interpret the data and sensor information to successfully complete his mission. A constant scan pattern is established by the pilot, both inside and outside the aircraft, and he manipulates the radar and FLIR in conjunction with the moving map and card files to fully exploit the aircraft's abilities to "see and strike" a target. The radar is used to verify the INS for position-keeping and target location, and is also used to "sanitize" the airspace for enemy fighters. The FLIR, NVGs and HUD are used to

Right: Busy moments on the 'Tigers" ramp at Cherry Point as ground crewmen await the signal to remove the wheel chocks from the aircraft. (Photo: Author)

Below: McDonnell Douglas show off the latest addition to the Harrier family. (Photo: McDonnell Douglas)

maintain a safe flight altitude, for terrain avoidance and for visual identification of targets. As the selected target is approached a final radar verification of the INS is accomplished, the weapons are armed and the area is once again "sanitized" for "bogeys". The aircraft then enters its predetermined manoeuvres for target ID, radar unmasking and threat reaction.

'The pilot is now centred on getting a good target acquisition, and getting his jet into the parameters for weapons delivery. Using a combination of radar, FLIR and INS, he acquires the target, and, using his computer delivery solutions, the ordnance leaves the wing pylons and heads for the target. The pilot pulls off, does a post-combat damage check on the hit and points the aircraft for home. The systems make it that simple.

'Setting up for landing, the NVGs are removed, unless the landing field is operating NVG-compatible lighting. Flaps and gear come down, the nozzles are rotated down and the airspeed decreases rapidly as the pilot continues to use his stick, rudder and throttles to control the aircraft. As the flight surfaces become ineffective due to loss of airflow, the reaction control "puffers" on the nose, wings and tail are opened up, using air siphoned from the engine. The pilot "stops" over his assigned landing spot and reduces power for a mild descent. Once on the ground, shut-down procedures are initiated and the pilot exits the Harrier, carrying with him his DSU, which now acts as a flight data recorder, backed up by a HUD video of the mission.

'The Harrier II Plus is a quantum leap for the Marines,' concludes Mike Richardson, 'as we now have the means to provide our troops with the fast all-weather response they need from us. The aircraft and what we can do with it continue to amaze me and we look forward to even greater achievements with the "Two Plus".

PHANTOM OF THE OPS

The silence of the the inky black night sky is broken by the rumble of turboprop engines droning even closer. From an observation position, a commander has called for some heavy, surgical firepower to deal with a convoy of enemy trucks moving along a road. Out of the darkness there comes the unmistakable sound of weaponry being brought to bear. Tracer rounds arc downwards, lighting up the ground as they impact. With unerring accuracy, a seemingly endless stream of fire thunders downwards on to the unsuspecting vehicles as an unseen hunter of the night plies its trade. This sort of power and precision can only mean one aircraft—the US Special Operations Command's AC-130 Spectre Gunship.

'We have the ability to loiter over a target and provide a continuous, concentrated wave of firepower, which makes us ideal for tight situations such as you might find in a CAS or interdiction role,' comments Captain Jerry Hicks, a member of the 16th Special Operations Squadron based at

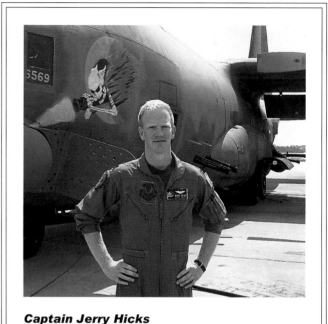

Captain Jerry Hicks
A very experienced Spectre pilot, Jerry Hicks is quick to confirm his admiration for his aircraft: 'It's an awesome machine.' (Photo: Author)

AC-130 Spectre Gunship

Above: Lockheed AC-130H Spectre Gunship (Photo: Lockheed)

Left: A Plane Captain gives his Spectre its final look-over before the huge beast taxies out. He is communicating with the crew via his intercom, the wire of which can be seen running into the open doorway. (Photo: Lockheed)

Hurlburt Field in Florida and a pilot of the lethal Spectre Gunship. 'We destroy. No other words for it—our mission is to kill the enemy and destroy his equipment, and we are very good at it. We generally operate at night, when we are less vulnerable to optical sensors; however, we still carry a fair amount of self-defence kit, such as ECM and chaff, but our main defence is the darkness. Here at the 16th the principle mission profiles we fly include night close air support, night armed reconnaissance and night interdiction, with, as you can see, the emphasis on the "night".

Based on the versatile Lockheed C-130 Hercules, the Gunship version is a product of the Lockheed

Aircraft Systems Company in Ontario, California. Built to meet an Air Force need during the Vietnam War, it was used extensively over the Ho Chi Minh Trail to find and destroy vehicles, and since its inception the Spectre has matured into one of the most specialized aircraft on the USAF's inventory.

The current variant of the Spectre is the AC-130H, which has been developed into a highly sophisticated side-firing weapons platform, designed to orbit a target, firing downward on to it, the idea being that the ordnance hits the centre of the circle—the target. To complete its tasks the AC-130H is fitted with an impressive array of weaponry and sensors. These include two 20mm rotary 'Gatling' guns, each capable of delivering 2,500 rounds per minute (which can be geared down to 2,000 rounds per minute) and primarily used for 'soft' targets. A single 40mm Bofors gun is also fitted, firing 100 rounds per minute, and is used against targets such as vehicles. The most potent weapon on board is a single 105mm Army howitzer

Left, top: The voracious twin 20mm guns . These are due to be replaced on the AC-130U by a single 25mm. (Photo: Mike Verier)

Left, centre: The 40mm gun, complete with flash suppressor. (Photo: Author)

Left, bottom: 'The Big Stick' on the Spectre is the 105mm Howitzer, capable of delivering up to six rounds per minute depending on the proficiency of the crew. Also visible here are the AN/APQ-150 beacon tracking radar and the powerful AN/AVQ-17 searchlight. (Photo: Author)

capable of dispatching between six and nine rounds per minute (depending on the efficiency of the crew), and this is used to strike 'hard' targets such as buildings. These guns are all fitted on trainable hydraulic mounts and 'tied in' to the ship's visual sensors.

'This "trainable mode",' says Jerry Hicks, 'allows us to attack targets in close proximity, without the pilot having to adjust the aircraft's position, but we are also able to operate them in a "fixed mode", which allows the pilot to acquire the target visually in an F-16 style HUD which is fitted to the left-hand window of his cockpit.'

The gun crews strive for a particular proficiency with their hand-loaded 105mms: they aim to have a shell in the breech, one on the way down and one hitting the target at any given time—'driving nails', in Gunship parlance. Because the howitzer points downward, the shell cases have to be specially crimped to stop them sliding down the barrel. Like the 105mm, which uses single rounds, the 40mm is also hand-loaded using four-round clips, and such is the appetite of the 20mm guns that one of the most important pieces of equipment aboard the Spectre is a 'snow shovel' to keep the spent cases from jamming up the breeches!

'The "brains" of the Spectre is the fire control system. It has two INSs, two fire control computers and a GPS, and these are tied into the Total Sensor Suite. This allows us to accurately navigate into an area and deliver our firepower in the minimum time from finding the target. We have two basic types of sensor, "visual" and "electronic". On the "visual" side is the AN/AAD-7 FLIR, which is housed in a ball turret beneath the undercarriage bay. This gives a 360-degree view and is primarily used to locate targets en route, and we are able to slave it to the INS to get a really tight position. Once we have found the target and established our orbit, we switch to our other visual sensor, the AN/ASQ-145V low light level television (LLLTV), which is mounted on an AN/AJQ-24 stabilized tracking set and fitted with an AN/AVQ-19 laser target designator and rangefinder. This equipment is located in the crew entrance door.

'The "electronic" sensors comprise an AN/APQ-150 beacon tracking sensor, which is essentially a SLAR (sideways-looking airborne radar) that searches for and acquires radar beacons from friendly forces. Once located, the signal from the beacon allows us to accurately fly to its location. It is also able to transmit data to us, updating our target information. Second is the AN/ASD-5 'Black Crow' sensor, which can be tuned to frequencies such as those transmitted by truck ignition systems. Also fitted is an AN/APN-59B search radar system (AGMTIP) in the nose, complete with moving target indicator (MTI), and external illumination is provided by a 2kW AN/AVQ-17 searchlight mounted in the aft cargo area, and this is capable of "normal" or infra-red operation. For self-defence we carry AN/ALE-20 chaff and flare dispensers fitted to the aft sections of the wheel bays, and wing-mounted SUU/42A pods which each fire chaff and flares. Additionally we can carry externally hung AN/ALQ-87 ECM pods if necessary.

'We carry a larger than average crew for a C-130: in all there are fourteen of us, five officers and nine enlisted men. At the front end are two pilots, a flight engineer, a navigator and a fire control officer

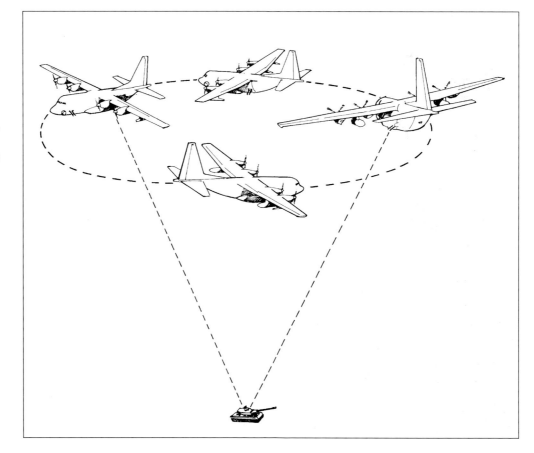

Right: The current variant of the Spectre is the AC-130H, which has been developed as a highly sophisticated side-firing weapons platform. The aircraft is designed to orbit its target, firing downwards on to it, the idea being that the ordnance hits the centre of the circle—i.e. the target. (Gavin McLeod)

(FCO, pronounced "Foco"). Two gunners normally man the 20mms in the back, and a third serves as a "right scanner" sitting just forward of "the booth", which is Gunship slang for the sensor suite compartment. Inside "the booth" is the infra-red operator, a dedicated electronic warfare officer (EWO) and the LLLTV operator. In the aft cargo compartment are two more gunners who man the 40 and 105mm "big guns", and finally, with his "bubble" at the rear, is the loadmaster, whose duties in a combat situation include looking outside and below the aircraft for any threats.

'Before any combat mission there is an intensive brief, where we look in as much detail as we can at our intended target or area of operations. The EWO is the recognized expert on all of the types of threat we could expect, and he will, together with the nav, plot our best route. We take an intel update and during our tasking evaluation we try to get a tight set of co-ordinates for our target so that we can be on station in the minimum time possible. When we get out to the aircraft, and unless it's the first trip of the day, it will have already been left "coked" by

Below: Captain Jerry Hicks checks out the HUD sight as he winds up his Spectre for another trip from Hurlburt Field. (Photo: Author)

Below right: A view inside the Hercules at the fire control officer's (Foco's) position. (Photo: Curtiss Knowles)

the last crew, so we literally start up and go. Mission call-signs are generally "Spectre", although we do use "Stinger" during local training trips. We carry enough gas for a five-hour sortie, and we are able to take addtional fuel from a tanker: 38,000 pounds is our normal loading, and we operate daily at our gross maximum weight. We are performance-limited because we carry a lot of high-drag devices, either sticking out or hung under the wings, all of which make it heavier and more difficult to fly than a "slick C-130".

'Also we must be the only attack aircraft in the world that goes into combat without ejector seats! However, we do have on board our own parachutes, and we all wear a parachute harness, lifejacket, survival vest and flying helmets, with NVG attachments. The gunners wear Kevlar helmets that offer greater protection against blast problems.

'Once airborne, we need to do a sensor alignment, so we orbit the field at a nominal altitude, say 6,000 feet, picking a single point on the ground and tracking it with the visual sensors. The Foco then aligns all of the ship's sensors to that point to ensure they are all "singing off the same sheet" and providing the correct information to the fire control computer. He also checks that the pilot's HUD is in the correct alignment. We then test our elements of geometry. In order for a Gunship to track and accurately hit a target, these elements need to work

together, and they consist of AGL, airspeed, and bank angle. An example would be 6,000 feet AGL, 172 knots' airspeed, and 22 degrees of bank. This enables us to fly an exact circle in space for the rounds to hit the target. We also evaluate the effects of two types of wind at this time, firstly the wind that affects the aircraft, and the ballistic wind that affects the trajectory of the round.

'Our next move is to "tweak" the guns, which is a check to ensure the round will impact where the sensors are looking. What we do is find a remote place and then fire off a flare, to give us a fixed position to work with. A "tweak" is one burst from each gun at 120-degree intervals, shooting three bursts from each gun in one orbit. For example, the first shot may be 3 mils forward or 3 mils low, so the Foco can input this to the fire control computer, until on the third burst it should hit the spot.

'On approach to the target area, we go to NVGs as the FLIR operator keeps a firm look-out to try and get an early target ID. At about 20 miles out, if we are working with a ground party we would give them a call up. Once contacted, we would authenticate them and have them give us an update. Crew co-operation is a big part of Spectre operations, and

Below: No 1 and No 2 guns, the 20mms, showing off one of the most important pieces of kit on the Spectre, a 'snow shovel', used to keep the mass of shell cases under control! (Photo: Author)

16th Special Operations Squadron
The 16th Special Operations Squadron became operational in 1968 at Ubon Royal Thai AFB as part of the 8th Tactical Fighter Wing, initially being equipped with the AC-130A but later with the more advanced AC-130E and H models. The Spectre was the deadliest of the night-flying weapons systems in Vietnam, accounting for an average of 10,000 trucks a year. In 1974 the unit moved to Korat AFB, from where it concluded its involvement in South-East Asia. December 1975 saw the 16th moving to its current home at Hurlburt Field as part of the 1st Special Operations Wing. Its next call to action was in Grenada in 1983, followed in 1990 by a spell in Panama, with a call to 'Desert Storm' coming later that same year. During the conflict the Spectres flew fifty combat missions, with the loss of one aircraft and her fifteen-man crew.

primary conversations are on two separate networks, plus the main interphone to which everyone has access. "Private 1" is used by the gunners, loadmaster and flight engineer, and "Private 2" is tactical and is used by the Foco, the EWO, the sensor operators, the nav and the pilots. If the EWO sees a threat, however, his transmission overrides all other conversations on board.

'About eight miles from the target we switch from "En-Route Guidance" to "Orbit Guidance", which will give us a tangent to the target as we roll in for our left-handed orbit around the area, using the attack mode segment of our orbit guidance system: this gives us a "circle" of flight and shows us left or right, fore or aft of the target. Once those are centred up and we are close to the nominal bank angle for the orbit, I look through the HUD and get a "diamond" superimposed over the target, which

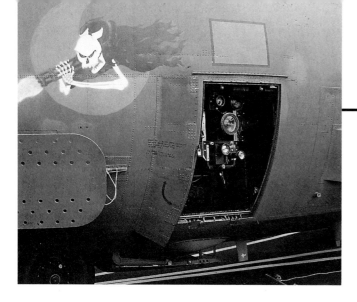

Above: Spectre symbols and door-mounted optics. (Photo: Mark Smith)

Below left: The navigator's position. (Photo: Author)

has now been acquired by the LLTV operator, slewing his sensor around by using a "thumbwheel" on his control panel. He "sparkles" the target with laser energy, allowing us to get an accurate track, and that allows the fire control computer to calculate the exact range. With all of the sensors now looking at the same point on the ground, the guns are set to "trainable mode", and these come up on

their hydraulic mounts. The sensor operator then keeps the target firmly fixed in the cross-hairs on his TV screen.

'The Foco now works in concert with the two sensor operators, known simply as "IR" or "TV"; he owns them, and he will have predetermined with them what he wants them to look for, and what he needs to see to convice him that a target is legitimate. The Foco then "calls" the target once he is sure, confirming trucks on the road. We have already planned to use our No 6 gun (the 105mm) to give them something to think about, so we approach. The gunners will have the weapons primed, with the shells ready, and as we roll into our orbit I call "Pilot in the HUD, arm the gun!" The Foco will have the No 6 gun selected on his panel, so he flips all his switches and sets the correct ballistics into the computer. In conjunction with the nav he again confirms the target and the flight engineer sets the master arm to "Live". In my HUD I get a CCIP, and I have to keep that CCIP in the trainable box, which ensures that the target remains in the gun's cor-

Above: One of the most menacing sights in the sky—a fully armed Spectre Gunship. This head-on view shows the aircraft's side-firing attributes. (Photo: Lockheed)

rectable parameters, so even in high wind I can still adjust the orbit to enable us to fire all the way round.

'When ready to shoot, I squeeze the trigger, and in "trainable mode" the last electronic link is to the sensor operator. When I have my finger on the trigger and all the constraints are met, he gets a "Ready to fire" light on his panel. He pushes a button, which is a momentary consent switch, and this passes the firing pulse to the guns, with the computer constantly checking the rate and coincidence. As soon as the round is out, I come off the trigger and the gunners "sling out the brass" and reload. They close the breech and call "Gun ready". I squeeze the trigger again. Meanwhile the sensor operators are looking at where the first round hits and making any adjustments for the next shell. When the 105 goes off it gives a pretty good jolt to the ship, but probably worse is a continuous burst from the 20 mil. This leaves a lot of smoke floating around, even in the cockpit, but as we have so many open spaces on board it soon dissipates.'

The Spectre is extremely good at its job, and it is combat-proven in conflicts from Vietnam to 'Desert Storm'. Because of the perceived need to provide its very special brand of firepower for many years to come, the AC-130H models are to be replaced with a new AC-130U, packed with more up-to-date sensors and more firepower—and making it the most vicious Hercules ever flown.

Left: The sign of the Spectre: Azrael, the Angel of Death. (Photo: Mark Smith)

'THE MAGIC'

Close air support is a demanding role by day, but providing precision CAS at night and in adverse weather is a completely different story, especially when the platform is a high-performance jet. Few aircraft are tailor-made for the role, but one in particular can boast that it possesses all the right 'tools', with a few unique wrinkles thrown in. The RAF's British Aerospace/McDonnell Douglas Harrier GR.7 is endowed with the latest sensor systems that enable it better to operate in the nocturnal environments of today's battlefield, and it is proving to be a real eye-opener for users and 'receivers' alike. These new systems are colloquially referred to as 'The Magic'.

'At night it is totally, totally different, and it amazes me just what we can see, and do, with this aircraft,' enthuses Squadron Leader Gerry Humphries ('Hum') of No 1 Squadron, based at RAF Wittering. 'At night time targets stand out better because of their thermal significance, and any lights showing can be seen up to 100 miles away! We can't be seen by most of the defences that threaten us in daylight hours—shoulder-fired SAMs, visually directed triple-A, small-arms fire, in fact anything that is command line-of-sight orientated is ineffective at night. Not that we are invulnerable—but we are much safer in the dark.'

At the heart of the Harrier's 'Magic' are a number of systems. The view into the night is provided by a GEC forward-looking infra-red system which is mounted ahead of the cockpit as close as possible to eye level, and its image can be projected on to either of the pilot's MFDs (multi-function displays) or directly overlaid on to his Smiths Industries wide-angle HUD, which continues to display all the visual flight data and navigational cues. Two modes are available for the FLIR, 'White Hot' and 'Black Hot', switchology being mounted on the throttle

Right: One of the main assets of the Harrier is its ability to operate from roads, car parks, rough field bases or forward operating sites. Here a grey GR.7 waits in a netted hide for its call to action. (Photo: BAe)

Above: Most of the needs of the aircraft can be catered for in the hides: even an engine change can be accomplished. (Photo: BAe)

Right: GEC Nightbird NVGs. (Photo: GEC)

(HOTAS) lever. A further feature of the FLIR is its ability to summon V-shaped symbol markers on to the picture, which draw the pilot's attention to any potential 'hot spots' such as vehicle engines. The FLIR is, however, limited by thick cloud because of the effect on the images created by water vapour.

The FLIR occupies a position at the top of a revised nose section on the GR.7, which also houses at its tip the glazed extremity of the Hughes AN/ASB-19(U) ARBS (Angle Rate Bombing System). Beneath the nose are two aerials for the Marconi ARI.23333 Zeus threat identification and jamming system, which is able to detect and jam hostile radar emissions using either a programmable net or a library of known threats. The system is also able automatically to dispense chaff and flares against such threats, with threat data capable of being displayed in the HUD or on the MFDs as well as by means of an audible warning.

The pilots routinely wear GEC Nightbird NVGs: with their excellent 40-degree field of vision, these complement the FLIR and are mounted on specially modified flying helmets which permit them to be swivelled upwards when not required and jettisoned from the helmet if the pilot needs to eject. The addition of GPS has also enhanced the aircraft's navigational accuracy: working in conjunction with the GEC-Ferranti FIN.1075 INS, this gives the aircraft a positional error of the order of a mere 30 metres.

It is late afternoon when the ATM is received at No 1 Squadron at its dispersed wooded site. The GR.7s sit in camouflaged hides on strips of PSP (pierced steel planking) and are being fussed over by anxious ground crews. The Harriers' VSTOL capabilities mean that they can operate from aus-

tere sites close to the FEBA, giving a superb response time and making them an invaluable CAS asset to the commanders.

'Our task is to attack fixed artillery positions that are shelling friendly forces,' explains Gerry Humphries. 'I will lead a pair of GR.7s against the sites and together with my number two set about planning our mission. First we look at exactly where the

Below left: The business end of 'The Magic'. Above the nose is the 'eyelid' cover for the FLIR, below that is the glazed aperture of the ARBS and beneath the nose are the twin aerials of the Zeus system. (Photo: Author)

Below right: Gerry Humphries adjusts the focus of his NVGs. Unlike their American counterparts, RAF pilots are qualified to make NVG take-offs and landings. (Photo: Author)

Squadron Leader Gerry Humphries

Born in Limerick, Ireland, Gerry Humphries joined the RAF in 1978 after completing a degree in aeronautical engineering at Queen's University, Belfast. Having flown some 180 hours on the Bulldog at his UAS, he followed the usual entry path through RAF Cranwell, ending up on the final Hunter course at RAF Lossiemouth flying the FGA.9. He moved to the Harrier in 1981 at Wittering and was subsequently posted to Germany and No 3 Squadron at Gütersloh. He then moved 'across the runway' to complete a further tour with No 4 Squadron. During 1986 he returned to the United Kingdom and joined No 1 Squadron at Wittering. He was given the task of starting up the RAF's Schools Presentation Team, travelling the length and breadth of the country to talk about air power to students. He returned to flying in 1991, again with No 1 Squadron, on the first GR.5 conversion course, and he was one of the first pilots to gain night qualifications with the new GR.7.

Above: The huge intakes of the Harrier are ideal for FOD ingestion, so care has to be taken when taxying out of rough sites. (Photo: BAe)

Right: A traditional 'green Harrier' in the field. (Photo: BAe)

No 1 Squadron
One of the oldest units in the RAF, No 1 Squadron has had a long association with the Harrier. Currently the Squadron is part of the RRF(Air)—Rapid Reaction Force (Air)—which is, at the time of writing, still in its infancy. This new challenge retains the unit's traditional CAS role, with particular attention to night operations, but combines it with a 'go anywhere' policy. Traditional commitments are to Norway, Denmark and Central Europe; however, with changing world events the Harrier Force has of late been operating in desert conditions in support of the United Nations operations over Iraq, flying from Incirlik AFB in Turkey.

Left: Grey scheme at the front end of a GR.7. (Photo: Author)

Right: Seen low over the coast of Wales, a single GR.7 lets fly with a salvo of SNEB rockets. (Photo: BAe)

target is located, and because we now have GPS we are very anxious to get the exact co-ordinates in the language the GPS understands. GPS operates in WGS84, whereas our maps are in OSGB, so an OSGB point is not exactly compatible with a WGS84. So we induce an error in the aircraft's computer to cater for this. We look at the terrain around the target, plus the known defences, and from that we work out our best attack direction, and our attack height. The ATM calls for a surgical precision strike, and, as the weather is beginning to deteriorate, a low-level attack is the most appropriate action, using CRV-7 rockets, which we can deliver with great accuracy without the need for a FAC on the ground.

'We look at approaches to the target to find the best chance of (a) not being hit, (b) seeing the target early enough and (c) getting an effective attack on the target and nothing else. Also I need to get film of the target, and using the CRV-7 means I can get coverage of the attack using my HUD camera, to use in later analysis. The low cloud base means that we have no moon and will be reliant on "cultural lighting", looking for the artillery to be active; if so, we should be able to pick it up from over 30 miles out.'

The configuration for the Harrier sees it toting two CRV-7 pods, underwing tanks, twin Sidewinder missiles, a Phimat chaff and flare dispenser plus two 'empty' ADEN cannon pods (these are retained to aid lift in VSTOL operations, the cannon not yet being cleared for use). Gerry Humphries picks up his kit, and, after a thorough mission brief and outbrief, he walks to his waiting Harrier. Walk-round checks complete, he climbs aboard and settles himself into one of the most modern cockpits available, and begins the arduous task of manually entering all the flight data into the computer using his UFC (up-front controller); he wears out a pair of gloves every two months, and the job will soon be undertaken by a data transfer system.

The Pegasus engine is wound up and, with all the necessary checks squared away, the camouflage netting is pulled aside and the Harrier Flight taxies out. Operating at such austere sites has its dangers, with any amount of FOD just waiting to be

sucked down the huge intakes. Using a rolling take-off, the aircraft are pushed to full power and amidst a storm of debris they clear the strip and climb away into the dusk sky. The pair join in battle formation and head for their first IP, after checking in on their Have Quick secure radio system.

With the weather closing in, the pair drop to 1,000ft, flying along valleys using the 'poor man's stealth techniques' and feinting runs in one direction before turning and re-entering from another.

'Hum' selects a 'Black Hot' image from his FLIR, which is projected on to the HUD. On his left MFD is the EW page of the computer display, and this is monitoring the threats. His moving map shows the aircraft approaching the first IP. On this occasion a large lake has been chosen as it stands out well as a thermal image.

'I check that "The Magic" agrees with what my eyes tell me . . . spot-on! If there were an error in the system, as we pass over the IP I could hit the WOF

Right: In-flight refuelling is possible by virtue of the Harrier's 'bolt-on' probe. (Photo: Author)

Above: Adopting a medium grey scheme for work over Iraq, the GR.7 demonstrates its abilities to carry a wide variety of ordnance. This particular example is carrying CBUs, Sidewinders, Phimat pod and centreline recce pod. (Photo: Andy Suddards)

Opposite, top left: The scene over the Moray Firth viewed through Gerry Humphries' NVGs. This photograph gives an excellent impression of 'cultural lighting' and shows how sensitive the goggles are. (Photo: Gerry Humphries)

Opposite, top right: With the FLIR set to 'White Hot' and projected into the HUD, this is the view of Wittering's main runway at the onset of a night sortie. The green world of the electronic systems contrasts with the 'normal' external lights at the edge of the picture. (Photo: Gerry Humphries)

Opposite, bottom: One of No 1 Squadron's commitments is to NATO's northern flank, and deployments are often mounted to Norway. This GR.5 is so deployed, complete with arctic camouflage. (Photo: BAe)

(waypoint over-fly) button and this pre-stores a range and bearing from that point which will again give an accurate update to the target. I make sure that all the switches are set live, the EW systems are active and the chaff and flares are on auto. The weapons sight in the HUD is giving me a distance to the target and a CCIP, height, speed and, most importantly, where the target is, indicated by a diamond symbol in the HUD.'

Racing into the target area, the pair perform a predetermined jink manoeuvre to ensure that if anyone on the ground is able to track them he will have an even more difficult task. As hoped, the flashes from the artillery tubes give away their positions, and 'The Magic' continues to identify other potential targets as the Harriers approach their fixed depression points. The FLIR is giving the crews a near-daylight image of the area as they come into range. The GPS has put them right in the slot and, using the CCIP, Gerry Humphries locks the target into his systems. 'Right on it,' he comments as the launch cue appears in his HUD. He squeezes the trigger and holds . . . The CRV-7s rip out of their canisters and stream to the target.

Looking under his NVGs, 'Hum' watches the missiles away and with a $5\frac{1}{2}$ g pull he rolls away from the debris hemisphere and picks up the egress route, his number two quickly following suit. The night attack was a success and the Harrier story continues—thanks to skill . . . and 'The Magic'.

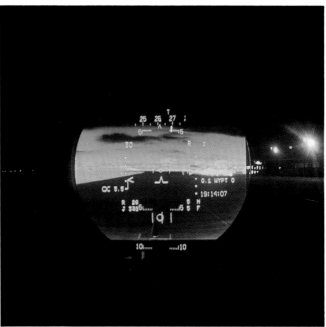

'SHAPE, SHADOW, SMOKE AND DUST'

'**H**ighlander Four-Four: [this is] Chalk Seven-Two. We have a target, grid Delta-Romeo-Two, thirty-two degrees, 1,500 to 2,000 metres down range, looks like a T-52 camouflaged in a woodline . . . Confirm.' In a momentary break from cover, a single US Army OH-58C Kiowa of the Air Cavalry calls in a strike on enemy armour. Highly trained eyes pick out the shape of a gun barrel from its surrounding foliage, betraying the position of the tank. At the controls of 'Chalk-72' is CW2 Roger Norris, and he and his scout helicopter belong to 'Charlie' Company, 2nd Battalion, 101st Aviation Regiment, 101st Airborne Division—the famous 'Screamin' Eagles'.

His 'confirm' call will be met by 'Highlander 44', an AH-64 Apache attack helicopter positioned some distance behind the scout, seeker and destroyer working in concert with a deadly purpose. 'Chalk-72 confirm' is the response as the Apache's hi-tech systems pick out and acquire the target. Soom laser-guided Hellfire missiles will be dispatched against it. Roger Norris ducks his little Kiowa back below the treeline and begins another sweep for enemy activity.

'Operating the OH-58C is the nearest thing you can get to flying like World War Two fighter pilots,' he explains. 'We are flying by the seat of our pants! No lasers, no optics, no sensors or any dedicated defensive armament. We rely on the traditional mark one eyeball, good tactics, a small, agile aircraft and excellent training. Most of our tasks see us operating in front of the main strike force, usually working for and with Apaches or Cobras, and we provide reconnaissance and close-in security for these high-value assets. The only deference we have to anything hi-tech in our "Charlies" is our NVGs for our nocturnal activities and latterly the fitment of Stinger air-to-air missiles, and these enhance our protection of the Apaches in our care.

'The Stinger missile fit has been a very effective addition to our aircraft. It was originally a shoulder-launched infantry weapon designed to combat low flying aircraft, but it is equally as good in the air-to-air role. The C model does not have the power to carry lots of weight, hence only two Stingers are mounted on the aircraft. Reloads can be carried in the rear; however, we are limited by the need to carry a nitrogen supply to cool the missiles' seeker heads.

'Within the 101st our principal tasks are air assault security, route reconnaissance, zone reconnaissance and deep strike reconnaissance, and during any recon mission we are the eyes and ears of the commander on the battlefield.

'We paint the picture for him while he is back at base, or he may be en route to the objective as we update the information. Another of our tasks is to provide spotting for the artillery: we take up overwatch or holding positions and then give them accurate fall of shot, and in return we use their barrage to cover us going in and coming out of the

CW2 Roger Norris
Flying the OH-58C is 'the nearest thing you can get to flying like World War Two fighter pilots. We are flying by the seat of our pants!' (Photo: 101 Airborne)

target area. We can also be used in the command and control mission, co-ordinating incoming "spot reports" from the battlefield and presenting them to the commander.

'In the battle zone (BZ) our chief responsibility is the close-in security of the Apaches. When they are engaged they will be looking way ahead at targets and therefore may not be aware of threats inside 500 metres, which is where the OH-58 excels. We protect their flanks and rear, looking for small-arms fire and any other threats, and we can employ our Stingers if an aerial threat arises.

'A mission for us begins with a Warning Order to the company commander. He calls together all of his "troops" and outlines the sorties we will be flying. He tells us that we need to prepare and gives us a time-on-target and take-off time. Crews then put together a detailed brief, which will include route, crews, tail numbers, laser codes, IFF settings and call-signs. A check of the weather, a final outbrief, pick up our kit and it's out to the aircraft. Most of our missions are at night, flying with the Apaches, but we also undertake daylight ops whenever we are called upon to do so.

'We like to fly our Scouts 'doors-off' a it gives us better vision and acts as air-conditioning during the hot summer months. However, this can get a bit uncomfortable in bad weather! The OH-58 is a small helo, with side-by-side seating in a very tight cockpit. The pilot occupies the right seat and his co-pilot/aerial observer the left seat. Our aircraft can be fitted with two Stinger missiles mounted on the starboard side, and to facilitate their operation the pilot has a PDU (pilot display unit) that hangs from the ceiling in front of him. This is basically a clear prism that gives him the symbology needed to fire the Stinger missiles. The PDU is essentially the same as that on the F-16 and gives arming and acquisition symbols as well as audible tones.

'On the right side console are the flight instruments; engine and transmission indicators are over on the left-hand console, as are the radios, which run along the centre console as well. It is a very neat

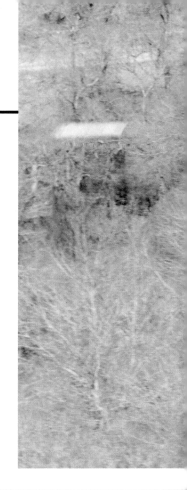

Right: An OH-58C Kiowa speeds across the treeline. (Photo: Bell Helicopters)

Below: A Kiowa flyer and his steed. The main sensors are 'the traditional mark one eyeball, good tactics, a small, agile aircraft and excellent training', and 'an innate suspicion of anything on the battlefield'. (Photo: Mike Verier)

Below right: The setting sun captures the atmosphere of the night scenario. Endowed only with night vision goggles and 'seat-of-the-pants flying', a Stinger-armed Scout heads into the dusk. (Photo: Mike Verier)

and compact working area. After engine start, which is by the old-style "twist-grip" throttle with starter button, we get a comms check and call in on our secure radios to let Lead know we are ready to go. We form up on the active runway, and Lead will turn through 90 degrees from the take-off direction and check the formation. Ten seconds from take-off he will call the code-word and go.

'Our route to target will be flown as low as possible and, dependent on the need, as fast as possible. Using predetermined de-confliction zones, we go out ahead of the Apache force, sometimes maybe as much as 30 miles in front, to give us the best possible opportunity of searching the route and BZ before their arrival. During our ingress we keep "comm-out" and only talk if there is a hazard to flight, as we are constantly on the look-out for

towers/wires or unmarked features that are at our altitude or higher.

'When we arrive at the BZ, tactics are to keep low, "pop up", evaluate and move forward to the next area. If we are happy, we can call across the Apaches. Because we have no optics, we have developed a visual scanning technique to cover the battlefield. We use overlapping fields of view, with a kind of "lazy-S" backwards-and-forwards movement, looking out from the aircraft in 50-metre overlapping intervals. The "acquisition sector" is 45 degrees off the nose, and we try to acquire targets as we progress or as they come into that sector. As they move to the left or to the right of our position, we call that the "recognition sector".

'Whilst in the BZ we could also be working with Air Force assets or with our artillery units, and for

the latter we have a standard "Call for fire" format. We give the location of the target, grid and description, plus method of engagement. The fire call would be "At my command" or "When ready", or a "Time on target". The FDC then comes back with what they intend to fire, who will fire, shell/fuse combination and number of rounds per tube. That gives me an idea of how long it will take, so I can mask and unmask at the right moment to observe the rounds hitting the target and keep moving. So, if he gives me a shot out with 35 seconds' delay, and because I know the distance from the artillery to the target, I would unmask in 20, get a good grid on the target, call "Splash" and get back down.

'On the battlefield we are on a constant look-out for "shape, shadow, smoke and dust": movement, lights, geometric figures etc. are all give-aways for us. If we spot something out of our field of view we call in the Apaches to use their long-range sensors to confirm the target. Much of our work is under the cover of darkness, and that's when the Apache really comes into its own. Night on the battlefield belongs to us, and although we have no optics the NVGs provide us with an excellent system to allow us to work. It enables us to fly low at relatively high speeds and lets us keep an eye out for threats that could hinder the progress of our forces.

'The OH-58 is an old aircraft now, yet it continues to be a superb scout for the Army. Being small does have its advantages: we are harder to hit, harder to see and, I suppose, a less expensive asset than the Apache! Our only defences are our flying abilities, experience, and an innate suspicion of anything on the battlefield.'

Left: Operating the OH-58C is 'the nearest thing you can get to flying like World War Two fighter pilots. We are flying by the seat of our pants' (Photo: Mike Verier)

Right: By comparison with the austere OH-58C, the 'Delta' model is a very different bird: with its mast-mounted optical and thermal sensors and Hellfire missiles it is very much an aggressor. (Photo: Mike Verier)

'THE PENETRATORS'

'The night and bad weather are our friends! Low cloud, poor visibility and no moon are all benefits to our operation. We take a lumbering, 175,000-pound aeroplane and fly it at heights of one hundred feet or lower through mountainous terrain in total darkness, hitting our assigned time on target to the second. We are the specialists.' Thus TSgt Mark Cunningham, a flight engineer, extols the virtues of the MC-130 Combat Talon II, which he flies with the 7th Special Operations Squadron at RAF Alconbury.

With due deference to the AC-130 attack and EC-130 electronic versions of the Hercules, the MC-130 flies the most demanding of mission profiles for such a large aeroplane, moving in hostile environments and undertaking clandestine operations. 'We have the task of being the Air Force's "penetrators",' continues Mark Cunningham. 'Our role is global by night or in adverse weather, and we have the ability to air-drop personnel and equipment, infiltrating or exfiltrating Special Forces and keeping them supplied in sensitive or politically denied areas.'

The MC-130 possesses some very high-tech equipment to fly these missions, and it is instantly distinguishable from other 'Hercs' by its unusual

7th Special Operations Squadron

Activated in 1942, the 7th SOS started life as the 27th Observation Squadron, and since this inception it has undergone a number of mission, nameplate and location changes. Following the Second World War it became the 7th Air Commando Squadron at Sembach AFB in Germany in 1964, acting as the principal special operations unit for CINCUSAFE. In 1968 the unit was redesignated the 7th SOS and moved to Ramstein AFB. In 1973 it again changed venue, moving to Rhien-Main AFB. Following outstanding contributions to 'Desert Shield' and 'Desert Storm', the unit deployed to the United Kingdom, and it currently operates from RAF Alconbury.

'duckbill' radome, which houses an AN/APQ-170 multi-mode radar, with ground mapping and terrain avoidance/terrain following capabilities. This allows the Combat Talon to fly low, 'picking holes through the terrain and threading through them like cotton through the eye of a needle'.

The cockpit and flight-deck work stations all have two video display terminals (VDT) together with data entry keyboards. Integral to each VDT are 21 variable-function, software-controlled switches positioned around the outsides. Key legends are shown on each VDT next to each switch, to indicate the current mode being displayed. The five switches along the top are for primary display modes, while the eight on either side provide the appropriate selection mode.

In the cockpit both pilot and co-pilot have two VDTs as well as the more traditional 'needles and dials'. These VDTs can show primary flight instrumentation as well as situational data. There are

Far left: Containing the TF/TA radar, the 'duckbill' radome of the Combat Talon II gives it one of the most recognizable features of any in the 'Herc' family. (Photo: Author)

Below: In full flow the Combat Talon is an impressive sight. (Photo: Cunningham)

Right, upper: On the flight deck of the Combat Talon II. The much-vaunted 'glass cockpit' is very much in evidence, with the four VDTs dominating the two pilot's positions. The VDTs display sensor and flight information as well as the TF/TA radar's 'bug' which allows the pilot to fly at such low levels in such a large beast. (Photo: Author)

Right, lower: The navigator's and EWO's positions, situated behind the pilot and flight engineer in the 'front end', are also dominated by VDTs. Currently displayed on one monitor is a very comprehensive FLIR picture, which can be shared by all the flight deck crew. The soft-touch function buttons can be seen around the outsides of the units. (Photo: Author)

Far right, upper: At the 'back end' the two loadmasters rig up a palletized cargo load for dispatch from the rear ramp. (Photo: Author)

Far right, lower: 'Down the rails': a cargo pallet is deplaned from the rear ramp. The High Speed Low Level Air Drop System (HSLLADS) used by the MC-130 allows the pilot to maintain a typical speed of 250kts at 250ft without the need for slowing or climbing to deliver the load (thus denying the enemy knowledge as to the exact location of the drop), and, in conjunction with the aircraft's computer-aided systems, makes for a very accurate delivery. (Photo: Author)

several varieties of vertical display formats for control of the aircraft, its guidance and flight information, with horizontal displays presenting tactical, radio and navigational data. These formats are available with symbology alone or can be overlaid with radar or FLIR information.

This complex beast is another Lockheed product. It is built by the company as a basic shell, with IBM Federal Systems Division handling the systems integration and E-Systems installing all the specialized avionics. For the degree of accuracy called for by its mission, the MC-130 has a dual INS and GPS which will be updated by an AN/ARN-92 LORAN-C. For the resupply function it is fitted with a Low Level Aerial Delivery and Container Release System, tied to a computer-controlled release point. Bad weather and night operations are further aided by the installation of a FLIR, fitted in a ball turret beneath the radome and enabling the crew to 'see' the world outside on their green VDTs.

'THE PENETRATORS'

Self-protection is enhanced by a large number of AN/ALE-40 chaff and flare launchers mounted on the wing pylons, fuselage and ramp. Also fitted are two AN/AAQ-8 infra-red countermeasures pods on the outer wing stations, together with an AN/AAQ-151R detection system, an AN/ALQ-172 detector/jammer, an ALR-69 radar warning receiver and an AN/AAR-44 launch warning receiver with its conical aerial fitted under the fuselage. All the cockpit and cargo areas of the Combat Talon have lighting that is compatible with the crew's night vision goggles—an "essential" for our operations.'

Compared with the 'task-staturated' Combat Talon I, the Talon II carries a crew of seven, two fewer than the earlier version. These are pilot, co-pilot, navigator, flight engineer, electronic warfare officer and two loadmasters. 'Crew co-operation is very high, but comms are low, due in no uncertain terms to the VDTs, which ensure we are all singing off the same sheet of music. The nav and EWO's VDTs give them an unrivalled ability to "see" the situation and the way ahead. The nav also controls the FLIR, the ground-mapping radar and the mission management and equipment status information. The EWO uses his VDTs to display the electronic warfare data and control all of the passive and active sensors and jamming equipment. He works very tightly with the nav at all phases of a mission.'

In the cargo hold of the MC-130 can be found more modifications, in the shape of the HSLLADS aerial delivery system. The rear ramp has been altered and the cargo floor strengthened to allow 22,000lb of cargo to be dropped from the aircraft while it maintains a 'normal' speed of 250kts at a height of 250ft, without the need for slowing or

Below: A 7th SOS Combat Talon II taxies out at the start of another training sortie over the Highlands of Scotland. (Photo: Author)

Above: Waiting at the 'hold point' for the main runway, an MC-130 runs up its four engines in preparation for take-off. The unique nose profile of the aircraft can be seen in this photograph. (Photo: Author)

TSgt Mark Cunningham
Originally trained on the 'vanilla' C-130 at Little Rock AFB, Mark Cunningham moved to the Combat Talon I and subsequently the Combat Talon II as an operational flight engineer, having spent two years on the Combat Talon II evaluation and test programme.

climbing, thus preventing the enemy from deducing the exact location of the drop. The loadmasters rig palletized cargo 'bundles' which are slung out of the aircraft's down-rails on the deck floor and ramp. This method negates the effects of wind and assures a direct trajectory to the target. The MC-130's computer system calculates all the drop parameters using the INS and GPS to come up with the necessary accurate co-ordinates.

'We are also now getting a refuelling capability that will add the type of mission scenario of the HC-130 to our list of abilities, and this has added another panel to my particular station. Once we have our tasking we put together a "team" of users for the flight. If it's a night trip we not only prepare the sortie but our body rythmns also—sleeping during the day, blacking out the windows, and working at night to plan the route and adjust our body clocks for the job in hand. We look literally at every inch of the plan: every aspect is scrutinized, and nothing, but nothing, is left to chance, taking on board all of the "what ifs?". When operating with any Special Forces we work in close liaison with them to ensure we haul to the exact co-ordinates they need. Once we are happy with the schedule we order up some tanker support to give us the "legs" for the trip; one or two prods might be in order, dependent on where we will be going. The pilots, nav and EWO generally have the in-depth knowledge of the mission, and they get together the rest of us for a full brief before we fly.

'Thirty minutes before take-off, the engines and electrics are fired up to give our complex systems a thorough check-out. As you could imagine, there is a high level of "challenge and response" flying around the cockpit. Once airborne and route-established, we would pick up our first refuel, usually

Left: The unique bulbous nose of the MC-130. (Photo: Author)

Above: Mounted under the nose is the all-important FLIR (Photo: Author)

Above right: Located at the furthest end of the Alconbury complex, away from the day-to-day hubbub of the base, is the home of the 7th SOS: 'We are less visible to the rest of the population, so if we have a task to perform we can move ahead with the minimum fuss.' As here, each Combat Talon is assigned a HAS position, spending all its time outside being 'mission-readied' (Photo: Author)

from a KC-10 or KC-135 out over the sea. Once tanked up, we position for the low-level phase, aiming for a coastal penetration at 100 feet. Using the ground-mapping radar, the nav picks out our minimum threat ingress, and maybe we would put in a feint and move further up the coast before turning back to our original heading. We favour poor/overcast conditions and mountainous terrain to mask our approach to the target, and by now the pilot is paying very close attention to his 890 lines of resolution on his VDTs. Displayed is the T/F radar's "cue" or "bug"; this is a circle cut through with a horizontal line, giving the pilot his attitude relevant to the terrain. Having already set the "clearance plane" above the ground, the pilot follows the "bug", making aggressive inputs to the controls to make sure we don't hit anything.

'Also displayed on his VDTs is the FLIR's image, along with temperatures, pressures, altitude, weights and engine performance. The T/F radar also works in turns: it "looks around corners" at the terrain ahead, which is comforting when we are flying down valleys with only 132ft clearance [the

wing span of the MC-130] to play with. With the pilot totally committed to his "zone of flight", it can get pretty interesting seeing features whizzing past the windows above our heads, especially through the green world of the NVGs. The nav is now in control of the show, and he is taking constant updates from the INS and GPS, and his route symbology is showing his exactly where we are in relation to the target—and he ensures the system remains 'tight'. Because of the high degree of automation, he does not have to rely on the traditional briefcase full of maps and charts.

'The nav and the EWO's VDTs give them an unmatched ability to see the situation and are able to present additional FLIR, navigation or EW scenarios to the pilot as they arise. As we approach the target zone, the loadmaster will prepare the back end and, at the signal, the cargo will be offloaded. With so many computer-driven systems on board, we are very proud of the accuracy and timing of our Combat Talons. We take pride in being able to hit our alloted TOT to the instant: 5–10 seconds late, and we are very disappointed! We aim for *zero*.'

145

'THAT OTHERS MAY LIVE'

'**W**e stand alert twenty-four hours a day, seven days a week, to rescue downed airmen or to offer assistance to civilian agencies should the need arise. Combat rescue is a demanding, challenging and hazardous occupation, but it gives you the super-high feeling, knowing that you have contributed to the saving of lives,' advises Lieutenant-Colonel Thomas Nolan of the 304th ARS, 939th Rescue Wing, AFRES, based at Portland International Airport in Oregon and operators of the latest recovery helicopter on the US Air Force inventory, the HH-60G Pave Hawk.

'We are the modern equivalent of the Jolly Green Giant of Vietnam fame, and we still operate the same "Sandy" combat rescue missions with covering fighters and tanker support. We transitioned to the HH-60G in 1991, and this helo has given us a much improved capability, due to its equipment

Below: A Pave Hawk crew working in concert to recover a casualty. The pilot hovers the aircraft while one of the PJs egresses the helo to assess, stabilize and recover the injured party. (Photo: Sikorsky)

status, its all-weather flying systems and, by virtue of in-flight refuelling, its extended range. Our principal mission is that of traditional combat search and rescue (CSAR) in the Pacific North-West, and as we are in close proximity to Mount St Helens, Mount Adams and Mount Hood, we assist the civilian community whenever we are called.'

The 939th's Pave Hawk is a product of Sikorsky Helicopters in Connecticut and is one of the 'high-tech' variants of the successful H-60 family, with perhaps the Blackhawk being the most abundant

type. Powered by two General Electric GE-700 turboshafts (due for updating in the very near future), the Pave Hawk is equipped with automatic flight controls and engine anti-ice systems that permit an all-weather capability. It carries a minimum crew of three, two pilots and a flight engineer, and, depending upon the mission, up to two pararescuemen. Self-starting is provided by an APU, which enables the crew to check out the sub-systems while the helo is still on the ground, and to enhance mission success further, the aircraft is

Lieutenant-Colonel Thomas Nolan
Thomas Nolan began his career in 1968 when he joined the US Marines. He started to fly in 1969 at NAS Pensacola, where he undertook basic flight training on the T-28, gaining his carrier qualifications aboard the USS *Independence*. Choosing the 'rotary route', he reported for HTA training at Elleson Field with Helicopter Training Squadron 8, flying the Sikorsky H-34. Once qualified, he moved to MCAS Santa Ana with the CH-46. During the Vietnam War he flew with Helicopter Medium Lift Squadron 364, the 'Purple Foxes'. When the Marines pulled out of Da Nang he moved to Iwakuni before returning to Santa Ana as an instructor. Leaving the Marines in 1973, he moved back to his home town of Portland, Oregon, and joined the 304th in 1974, flying the hoist-equipped UH-1 until the advent of the Pave Hawk. During his time with the 304th he was involved with the rescue efforts following the Mount St Helens eruption.

fitted with a Bendix weather radar mounted in a small radome on the starboard side of the nose, a GPS and a centrally mounted FLIR. A flight re-fuelling probe is located on the port side of the nose and two extra internal fuel tanks holding 24,000lb of gas have been added, giving the Pave Hawk an unrefuelled range of 504 miles. Above the star-board crew door is a rescue hoist which carries 200ft of cable and is able to lift 600lb at any one time. An underslung cargo hook is also available.

The crews routinely use NVGs for operations as the HH-60 is endowed with compatible cockpit lighting. For self-protection, chaff and flare launch-ers are fitted, along with two door-mounted M-60 machine guns. However, unlike its sister-type, the MH-60G used by the Special Operations flyers, the HH-60G does not have the external stores systems (ESS) pylons fitted.

'The two pilots up front are separated by a con-sole that rises to the rear of their seats, making it impossible for them to enter the rear cabin. The flight engineer sits behind the right-hand pilot: he has responsibility for most of the radios and he operates the hoist as well as being the primary scanner. Behind the left-hand pilot is another seat that is occupied by one of the para-rescuemen or "PJs". He also acts as scanner, and both the PJ and the flight engineer are able to operate the door-mounted guns. On a normal CSAR mission we would also carry a second PJ in the rear cabin; one of these would be the team leader, the other the primary medic. The "PJs" are trained in rapelling and fast-rope techniques as methods of quickly exiting the helicopter to get aid to any survivors, and they also hold an EMT National Medical Rat-ing. They have the expertise and technical know-ledge that goes with the medical and specialist rescue equipment we carry. The second PJ's role in the rear cabin is to assist his colleague, either on the ground stabilizing the casualty or in the helo manning the weapons or helping with the hoist work.

'Because of the extra fuel tanks fitted in the rear cabin, the maximum number of litters we can take is two, which at first glance makes us look rather small, but we have traded space for range and endurance—the difference between life and death in some circumstances.

Above left: The main features of the HH-60G are the IFR probe (left), the FLIR (centre) and the weather radar (right). (Photo: Scott)

Left: The 304th 'team': TSgts Hacklet and Villasenor, Colonel Nolan, TSgt Schulte, SSgt Barker (crew chief) and SMSgt Morris (flight engineer). (Photo: Scott)

Above: The large crew access doors on all models of the Blackhawk family are a real bonus for the SAR role of the Pave Hawk. (Photo: Curtiss Knowles)

'On a CSAR mission, once we have been advised that an aircraft is down, usually by the Joint Task Force Commander, we prepare to mount our rescue. One of the first things we establish is the size of the "Alert Package". The Alert Package comprises the HH-60s (we retain the "Jolly" call-sign), the aircraft playing the "Sandy" role, usually F-16s or A-10s, plus any other assets that may be needed to penetrate hostile airspace, e.g. Wild Weasels and tankers. Intel come in with their synopsis of the situation, the position of the aircraft down, and their recommendations. From this information we formulate our route and altitude, which is dependent on exactly what is in the area. We then prepare our maps and charts and make ready coordinates to punch into the aircraft's GPS. Depending on the

304th Rescue Squadron
The 304th Rescue Squadron is part of the 939th Rescue Wing located at Portland International Airport in Oregon and belongs to the United States Air Force Reserve (AFRES). The unit provides a twenty-four-hours-a-day, seven-days-a-week alert status in the Pacific North-West and is involved in both military combat search and rescue and civilian rescue missions.

prevailing situation, we will be given a time to launch, which could be anything from a half-hour to up to two hours away.

'Once we are airborne we are co-ordinated by AWACS, and, again depending on the threats, we may go direct to the survivors or take a route that keeps us away from any threats. Once in the area we either make a direct approach or hold and wait to be called in by the "Sandys" once the area is clear. The actual mechanics of a retrieval depend on a number of factors such as the survivors' condition, how long we might be on the ground, threats, terrain and the weather. If there are threats in the

Below: An HH-60G from the 304th overflies Reed Glacier during an SAR exercise in 1994. (Photo: Scott)

Right, upper and lower: Para-rescuemen (PJs) are trained to cope with overland and underwater situations. (Photo: Scott)

area we might want to fast-rope the PJs and exit to a safe distance till they have packaged up the survivors for us to come in and collect, or maybe because of deteriorating weather conditions we will want to stay on the ground, to avoid having to fly back into a storm. Once the survivors are stable, we head back out by the safest route to base.'

It is not only the aircrew who experience a hazardous mission: the PJs are also amongst 'the élite'. TSgt Richard Konopka explains: 'To be a PJ is an intensive and all-consuming way of life. The para rescue selectees go through a twelve-week indoctrination course at Lackland AFB in Texas, where they learn the basics of the job. They move to Airborne Infantry Training at Fort Benning in Georgia, where they are taught static-line and military parachuting, and from there it's off to the Special Warfare Center at Fort Bragg in Carolina and Key West where they learn scuba diving and water skills before attending the US Air Force Water Survival School at Tyndall AFB. They then go to the Land Survival and Resistance Training School at Fairchild AFB, where they learn food and water procurement and evasion techniques as well as simulated POW camp experience. They then return to Fort Bragg for a six-week parachutist course.

'These are the prerequisites for these men, and once all this has been achieved they move to the actual para-rescue training at Kirkland AFB in New Mexico, where they spend ten months in the programme. The first six months are for Emergency Medical Technician training at paramedic level, and after that there are field operations, which feature mountaineering, navigation and environment survival, followed by the Tactics Phase with small teams, simulated combat manoeuvres and aerial operations, learning to parachute with scuba gear and how to be a crew member on fixed and rotary-wing aircraft. After this gruelling course the trainees will be awarded their basic level certificate and dispatched to a unit for on-the-job training and any specifics that unit may practise.

They also attend a "Snow and Ice School" and Advanced Weapons, Aerial Gunnery, Dive Rescue, Dive Medical and SAR Management training, plus other specialist courses that are essential for the job. It is also worth noting that all air crews undergo land and water survival training as well as the simulated POW camp, to prepare them for the rescue mission.

'Here in the north-west in Oregon we are also tasked with supporting NASA's Space Shuttle programme as well as our own civilian SAR, and the latter has seen us operating over glacier-covered

Above: The Pave Hawk/HC-130 Hercules combination at work en route to a 'rescue'. (Photo: Scott)

volcanoes and mountainous terrain which in itself brings a unique set of problems.'

Co-located with the 304th at Portland is the 301st ARS with its HC-130 tankers. 'We rely on these guys to give us our legs,' comments Thomas Nolan, 'plus they undertake portions of missions that we may be unable to swiftly achieve. They fly high and fast, we fly low and slow, so they are able to quickly get PJs into a situation that may be critical. If we had to respond to a ship 400 miles off the coast, the HC-130s could leave with the PJs and drop them with a Zodiac boat into the water and orbit the scene till we arrive, topping up our tanks for the return journey while the PJs attend to the problem. They are also useful in providing command and co-ordination, and equally useful are their beacon trackers that can help pinpoint downed airmen. We are a very good team.

'"That others may live" is our motto in rescue,' concludes Thomas Nolan. 'It is a privilege to serve in the CSAR mission.'

AIR GUARDS

The Boeing E-3D Sentry, designated Sentry AEW.1 in British service, encompasses true 'state of the art' technology and gives the Royal Air Force the capability effectively to patrol the United Kingdom Defensive Air Region (UKDAR). It is also an integral part of NATO's early warning strategy. The RAF's involvement with airborne early warning began in 1977 with the transfer of responsibilities from the Royal Navy (which flew shipborne Gannet AEWs). The re-formed No 8 Squadron, equipped with the piston-engine Shackleton, took on the task by fitting out its aircraft with the Gannet radomes and radar systems. Originally planned as an 'interim' solution, the Shackleton was envisaged as having a short service life, and in order to fulfil the role in the long term the British Government laid plans to develop an indigenous AWACS aircraft based around the proven Nimrod maritime reconnaissance aircraft. In 1977 work began to convert eleven Nimrod airframes to a new AEW.3 standard, which included radical tail and nose radomes which gave the aircraft a rather 'bulbous' appearance.

The conversion and flight-testing of the airframe changes were successful, but the radar and computer systems were dogged with problems, and despite time extensions and extra money being made available to bring the AEW.3 to operational status, it became clear that the whole project would be unable to meet the RAF requirements and the programme was cancelled in 1986. The Government's attention then centred around the proven Boeing E-3, already in service with the USAF and NATO. At the same time the French Air Force, also in the market for an AWACS, and expressed an interest in a joint purchase of E-3s tailored to suit the individual air forces' requirements.

Following discussions, the two Governments announced a combined purchase comprising seven air-

Right: The 'eyes' and the 'teeth' of the United Kingdom's aerial defence: the E-3D Sentry and the Panavia Tornado F.3—a deadly combination. (Photo: BAe)

craft for the Royal Air Force and three (with an option on a fourth) for the French Air Force. The first RAF E-3D, ZA101, was rolled out in June 1989 and No 8 Squadron, then based at Lossiemouth in Scotland, moved south to Waddington during June 1991 to take charge of their new aircraft. The final E-3D, ZA107, was the 1,000th and last of the Boeing line.

'The Sentry AEW.1 is built around the military version of the Boeing 707-320B commercial airliner,' explains Flight Lieutenant Steve Larry, a Sentry pilot with No 8 Squadron at RAF Wadding-

Above left: The wingtip-mounted Loral 'Yellowgate' ESM pod and rearward-facing HF aerial. (Photo: Author)

Above: Detail on the 30ft rotodome. (Photo: Author)

Left: The Sentry's flight deck. (Photo: BAe)

Above right: The RAF's two heavyweights, the Sentry and the TriStar, both showing their airliner heritage. (Photo: Author)

Far right: The E-3's rotodome contains not only the radar scanner but also the IFF and data-link systems. The two pylons that carry the rotodome contain electrical power, microwave waveguide ducts and cooling pipes. Power cables snake across the Waddington pan; note the specialized 'dollies' that carry them. (Photo: Author)

ton, home of the United Kingdom's Airborne Early Warning Force. 'The aircraft contains all of the basic E-3 components, many of which have been improved the suit the RAF's requirement for greater coverage in the maritime regime. We also have the quieter and more fuel-efficient General Electric/ SNECMA CFM56-2A-3 turbofan engines complete with thrust reversers, a fact which is much appreciated by the Waddington residents, who only a few years ago had the very noisy Vulcan bombers on station! Also our operating height is a significant improvement over the old Shackleton, as now we fly at 30,000 feet compared to 5–8,000ft in the "Shack". Endurance is improved and crew comfort is also much better, as we can stay aloft for eleven hours unrefuelled, and this can rise to 20–24 hours with IFR, which incidentally can now be achieved either from drogue-equipped tankers such as the RAF uses or boom-equipped tankers from the USAF—a dual "first" on any RAF machine.

'Perhaps the most striking feature of the E-3 is its 30ft-diameter rotodome which houses the radar antennae, IFF and data links. The radar gives us a 360-degree field of view, allowing us to observe targets more than 200 miles away, and we can

Left: High over the North Sea, an RAF Sentry transits to a patrol location. (Photo: Author)

Below left: E-3D Sentry AEW.1. (Photo: Author)

Right: The dim interior of the RAF's E-3 Sentry, showing the consoles and display terminals. (Photo: BAe)

Below right: The RAF's E-3D Sentry is unique in that it is the Service's only type that is able to refuel from both drogue- and boom-equipped tankers. Also in view here are No 8 Squadron's honorary 'fighter bars' behind the crew access door. (Photo: Author)

detect and track air and sea targets at the same time. The data-link is known as "Link-11" and it provides a "god's-eye view" of what the aircraft's systems are detecting. We then are able to share what we have on our screens with ground stations, fighters and warships that we are in contact with to provide the "big picture".

'We carry a crew of seventeen, but unlike our colleagues in NATO who operate a "soft crew" format, drawing on available personnel as required, our crews fly regularly together as a team. We have four flight-deck crew, three NCO airborne technicians who look after the systems while we're in the air, with the remainder of the officers coming under the authority of the Tactical Director, and they all work in the windowless, low-light world of the main fuselage. There are three rows of consoles set at right angles to the aircraft's body (and these make nine working positions in all), and these are backed

No 8 Squadron RAF
Formed on 5 January 1915, No 8 Squadron operated in France, Egypt, Iraq and Aden up to 1945. During the Second World War it flew as a bomber unit with Blenheims, Marylands and Hudsons, finishing the war with Wellingtons and Liberators. No 8 had the honour of being the last front-line operator of the Hunter, disbanding on the type in Sharjah in 1971. Since then the unit has been associated with the airborne early warning role, flying the Shackleton AEW.2, the RAF's last front line propeller-driven aircraft. No 8 converted to the E-3 Sentry in 1991.

by a communications station manned by two crew and a systems station which monitors all the complex computer systems and "black boxes". In the rear we have a well fitted-out galley, bunk beds and airline-style seating.'

At the time of writing the RAF's E-3 force is heavily involved patrolling the skies of Bosnia in Operation 'Deny Flight', and although there is now a new openness between East and West, the Sentry is a reassuring asset, keeping a watchful eye over unfolding events.

Below: Inside its protective compound, an E-3D is prepared for flight, with a plethora of ground equipment in the foreground. (Photo: Author)